"It's one thing to read a mov and recovery, but quite anoth .... your eyes. Such is the role I've had with the Vallotton family since the day their world collapsed. This great family got just what they didn't deserve. The unbelievable pain was paralyzing. Yet turn after turn, they moved redemptively and discovered God's goodness in a new way. *Winning the War Within* gives us exactly what we need: honesty, inspiration and insight to enable us to understand the process to health and recovery. Both Jason and Kris have an unusual gift to communicate through writing. This is a much-needed book in the library of every believer."

Bill Johnson, senior leader, Bethel Church,
Redding, California

"Jason Vallotton, along with his father, Kris Vallotton, are laying the foundation to incredible freedom and joy in their book *Winning the War Within*. This book is unashamedly honest and challenges you to look at your own heart with the same honesty. We completely believe this book will set the captives free and heal the brokenhearted! It not only teaches you how to forgive but also how to walk it out and see it through to completion in your life. *Winning the War Within* will bring greater intimacy with the Father to every heart that embraces it."

Kim Walker-Smith and Skyler Smith, Jesus Culture

"*Winning the War Within* is much more than a set of principles, a fresh Bible study or even a powerful testimony. This book is a piece of the Vallotton family's heart. In a beautiful context and style, Kris and Jason pen some of the most painful experiences of their lives. The unique approach of this book on forgiveness and pain is the paradigm in which they lived the unfolding events. I encourage anyone seeking to learn a supernatural response to betrayal, offense or broken relationships to read this book and be forever changed."

Danny Silk, author, *Culture of Honor*
and *Loving Our Kids on Purpose*

"We are all on a journey in this life, and we each have a story to tell. Our stories include everything, whether it is good, bad or ugly. When we engage with one another, we learn how to walk in each other's shoes. The testimonies we hear give us power to do the same things with the same results. I know Jason's story. I have a similar journey. I appreciate anyone who can turn pain into a radical process of becoming like Jesus.

"It is in the valley that our lives are truly adjusted to the pleasures of God. On the mountain we have sovereign encounters with majesty and beauty, and then we must return to the scene of the devastation and begin to plant what God has sowed into us. This is where we encounter the incomparable delight of the Comforter, who steps into our devastation with His own gracious touch and renovates us from the inside out.

"Forgiveness that is etched in grace creates a lifestyle of loving that is powerful, releasing and effective. All who read this book will be changed, because they will be drawn into the story of Jesus walking with beauty in the fields of pain."

Graham Cooke, author, speaker and publisher

"There are libraries full of books that can fill your head with knowledge and facts, but then there are those special books that transcend information and have the power to transform your life. *Winning the War Within* is one of those books. I am so grateful for the way Jason and Kris have dared to open up their own lives and give us this special book."

Jonathan Helser, worship leader;
co-director, 18 Inch Journey and Cageless Birds

WINNING THE WAR WITHIN

WINNING THE WAR WITHIN

THE JOURNEY TO HEALING *and* WHOLENESS

JASON VALLOTTON
with
KRIS VALLOTTON

Chosen
a division of Baker Publishing Group
Minneapolis, Minnesota

© 2011, 2020 by Jason Vallotton and Kris Vallotton

Published by Chosen Books
11400 Hampshire Avenue South
Bloomington, Minnesota 55438
www.chosenbooks.com

Chosen Books is a division of
Baker Publishing Group, Grand Rapids, Michigan

Printed in the United States of America

ISBN 978-0-8007-9973-1

Library of Congress Cataloging-in-Publication Control Number: 2019050969

Portions of this book previously published by Regal Books in 2011 and Chosen Books in 2014 under the title *The Supernatural Power of Forgiveness*.

Unless otherwise indicated, Scripture quotations are from THE HOLY BIBLE, NEW INTERNATIONAL VERSION®, NIV® Copyright © 1973, 1978, 1984, 2011 by Biblica, Inc.® Used by permission. All rights reserved worldwide.

Scripture quotations identified ESV are from The Holy Bible, English Standard Version® (ESV®), copyright © 2001 by Crossway, a publishing ministry of Good News Publishers. Used by permission. All rights reserved. ESV Text Edition: 2016

Scripture quotations identified MESSAGE are taken from *THE MESSAGE*, copyright © 1993, 2002, 2018 by Eugene H. Peterson. Used by permission of NavPress. All rights reserved. Represented by Tyndale House Publishers, Inc.

Scripture quotations identified NASB are from the New American Standard Bible® (NASB), copyright © 1960, 1962, 1963, 1968, 1971, 1972, 1973, 1975, 1977, 1995 by The Lockman Foundation. Used by permission. www.Lockman.org

Scripture quotations identified NKJV are from the New King James Version®. Copyright © 1982 by Thomas Nelson. Used by permission. All rights reserved.

Note that in some of the authors' stories, the names and identifying details of certain individuals have been changed to protect their privacy.

Cover design by LOOK Design Studio

20 21 22 23 24 25 26   7 6 5 4 3 2 1

Contents

Contents

Foreword

This book is a powerful key to unlocking the hearts of those who have been trapped by the pain and memories of their past traumas and experiences. Jason's vulnerable testimony will help those who have been hurt and betrayed to find the courage and strength to face their own pain. His journey of love and forgiveness testifies that there is no situation beyond the unending reach of God's love and redemption. God promises us that if we give Him the ashes of our lives, He will exchange them for His beauty, no matter how big our ash heap seems to be!

Jason and Kris have shared deep insights from the heart of God that are crucial for the journey from pain into the beauty of His restoration. They have done an amazing job of writing about a difficult subject in a very transparent and moving way. Their openness and vulnerability will pave the way for many to come out of the prison of unforgiveness and into a place of healing and freedom.

During the last several years of being a missionary in one of the poorest nations in the world, I have seen some of the greatest suffering imaginable. I have also had the joy of seeing God bring about restoration in the most remarkable ways! This hinges on one of the biggest decisions that we can ever make: the decision to forgive. Forgiveness makes the difference between continued torment and suffering, and freedom and redemption beyond our wildest dreams.

Often, I have witnessed how those who have experienced unimaginable atrocities have come into a radical transformation beyond what they could have ever hoped for. This happened as they courageously chose to forgive. One such person is Luis. He is one of my greatest heroes. He taught me about the power of forgiveness and mercy.

I found Luis on the streets. He was sick and full of anger because he had been burned in his house (which was a cardboard box) by people who had previously been his friends. They had poured gasoline on it, tied him to the cardboard and lit it on fire, leaving him to die. He was terribly burned and spent many months in a dilapidated local hospital. He was unhappy and bitter about being treated so horribly. His misery had brought him to a place of great brokenness, and he had nothing left to take pride in. He would often wet himself, and he lived in filth.

When I met Luis, I held him in my arms and told him about Jesus' passionate love. I invited him to come home and live with us. At the time, Luis was not very merciful or forgiving; he made his living by hitting, stealing from and knifing people! But I kept telling Luis about this man named Jesus who had given up His home and riches and had walked the streets—the One who had left heaven and came to earth to find him. Eventually, Luis said, "I must know this man!"

One day, Luis came to me and said that he wanted to go to the streets with me so he could tell the guys who had tried to kill him that he forgave them. I watched Luis pour out extravagant mercy on many in the streets of Maputo, and I watched the favor of God increase in his broken little life.

One of our churches at that time was an unconventional congregation. We met in a brothel to reach the prostitutes. We worshiped Jesus, prayed and simply loved the resident prostitute girls. We were not seeing a lot of breakthrough, however, in the girls escaping the cycle of their destructive lifestyles. (Some of these girls were as young as ten, eleven and twelve years old, and they were selling their bodies on the streets for a bottle of Coke.) I was desperate for Jesus to set them free.

While I was on a 40-day fast (and feeling very hungry and desperate), I cried out to God to change the situation. Shortly after this, the girls fell on their knees during worship and started screaming, "We cannot sell ourselves anymore!" I started weeping for joy and asked Jesus what I should do next. I knew that I could not move these girls into the same center as the boys and that I needed to find a church where the pastor would not fall into temptation. I needed a pastor whose heartbeat matched Jesus' in holiness and purity, and who was free from judgment.

After crying out to God, I looked up and saw Luis praying and worshiping God wholeheartedly in the dirt. He had not finished the pastors' Bible school because he could not read or write, but he was a man full of mercy and compassion. Luis was worshiping with his hands lifted up, adoring the Lord. I held Luis and asked him if he would like to care for these girls as a pastor. He fell apart sobbing, asking if God could give him the privilege and honor of such a beautiful task.

Kneeling down, he looked up at me and asked, "Could God have such great love to use a man like me?" Luis had great humility and great love! He moved to a small new base and began to pastor the girls.

Luis is in heaven now. He died of the AIDS he had contracted in his youth, while living on the streets. Luis's life was one of love, mercy and radical forgiveness, poured out in worship for his King. This day, in heaven, he is full of joy with his Bridegroom. "Blessed are the merciful, for they shall receive mercy" (Matthew 5:7 NASB).

Jason and Kris, like Luis, have chosen to let go of the ashes of their deep pain and have said a costly yes to God's great exchange. They have chosen to walk in ultimate justice where forgiveness and releasing is the standard of righteousness, rather than bitterness and revenge. I am so proud of the Vallottons and the way that they have walked in love through an extraordinarily difficult situation. I have watched their lives and have witnessed firsthand how they have chosen to forgive and to show extraordinary compassion.

This is ultimate justice: that even in our times of deepest pain, we get the privilege of partnering with God in His boundless love and get to experience the height, breadth and depth of His glorious forgiveness flowing through us to others. This is the highest call imaginable and the greatest ministry conceivable, and it is for all of us. It is the call and mandate to love so deeply and so well that it will turn the world upside down!

Heidi Baker, Ph.D., founder and president,
Iris Global, www.irisglobal.org

Introduction

I never dreamed that any of my children would come to me and break the news that my son Jason did the day he visited my office several years ago. And I never imagined that what he had to tell me would trigger one of the worst nightmares in our family's history. Nonetheless, I sat there, stunned, trying my best to absorb his words.

"Dad," he said, "I think my marriage is over."

For the next eighteen months, I watched my son writhe under the intense pain of rejection, abandonment and grief. Day after hard day, I stood by my family as we mostly fumbled about trying to make sense out of the unfathomable.

My wife, Kathy, and I did our best to comfort our family, but we were wounded, too. It felt as if we had been harpooned in the very depths of our own souls. I had lost my father when I was three years old and had two stepfathers who abused me, but I had never experienced pain like this. Together we cried enough tears for a lifetime.

As we plodded on, something profound began to emerge. It started with Jason, the most wounded of all. As he struggled through the healing process, he received incredible insights. He would say things like, "Dad, God showed me that it's only when we mourn that we are comforted." Jason chose to embrace his pain instead of run from it. At first I questioned the validity of his wholeness. I thought he was living in some sort of denial to help him cope with his extraordinary grief.

As time passed, however, I came to realize that he had taken the most unusual path to wholeness that I had ever seen. Not only was his revelation unusual, but it was also working. Jason and our family were getting well, and joy was filling our lives once again.

The idea of facing pain head on and coming out the other side filled with true joy may be foreign to many Christians, who out of fear succumb to the religious peer pressure of putting on the mask of a happy face at all times. Consequently, hurting people push down their pain instead of confronting it. This leads to a life of unresolved agony, as bleeding hearts continue to fester and never receive the comfort needed to truly heal. Our culture tends to avoid pain because many of us have never been given the tools to work through heartbreak and come out the other end of the process healed, whole and healthy.

In the midst of his grief, Jason started processing his thoughts through journaling and songwriting, which led him to create a toolbox for working through his pain instead of trying to leap over it. Once in a while he would sing me one of his songs or read me something he wrote. His journal was filled with amazing wisdom and deep insights into the process of his wholeness. He began using his new tools as he ministered to people in our ministry school and church family. Before long he was helping hundreds of people find keys to unlock their own prison doors of pain. When he shared his journey from the podium, people lined up to tell him their own stories and then listen to his wisdom. Now Jason shares his insights and wisdom in this book.

A family psychologist did not write *Winning the War Within.* Instead it was penned by two people—a son whose heart was broken into a million tiny pieces when his marriage ended, and by his father, who healed alongside him.

The insights came to Jason, and he is the one who lived them out, so he writes most of the book. I added a chapter of my own and insights and reflections in some of the others. Our prayer and sincere desire are that the words of this book would become your path to wholeness and joy. May God Himself meet you as you read and lead you into the palace of your dreams.

Kris Vallotton, father of a restored family,
www.krisvallotton.com

Preface

The Story of a Thousand Lives

From the beginning of our creation, we were designed to win every battle, war and conflict—regardless of the cards we were dealt. Our history in God proves this over and over. With a little faith and some jars, trumpets and torches, three hundred men defeated an army so large that it was impossible to count all the opposing warriors. In Sunday school we learn about Daniel in the lions' den and about David slaying Goliath with a single stone and no fear. Yet when it comes to us, we crumble at the first sight of opposition because we have not conquered our inner fears.

I am no different from the rest of humanity. My story is the story of a thousand lives. White picket fences and clean sidewalks were my fortress, protecting me from the evils of a world gone mad. I walked the thin line of safety, struggling to weigh out each decision, knowing that each had the potential to affect my eternity. Yet, as careful as I was, heartache somehow found its way to my front door, leaving me emotionally broke and physically devastated.

Over the past fifteen years of being a pastor, I have heard a myriad of stories from people from all different walks of life. Most of these situations you would never wish on your worst enemy. But with each story (including mine) I have found a golden thread interwoven among them all.

What we learned in school taught us how to climb the ladder of intellectual success. Academically we have been carefully groomed to position ourselves for promotion, with the mindset that a person's happiness lies in his or her ability to create monetary success and financial stability. I have found, however, that regardless of all the scholastic training and philosophical lectures, people are still left hurting, wondering how to do real life. In spite of the countless hours of teaching, even from our mothers and fathers, we have no idea how to navigate the world we live in. Disappointment, pain and fear have so ravished our society that we now live in the most medicated time in history, with no end in sight!

It is in my heart to lead others back to the freedom from hurt in which God created them and encourage them to be powerful in every situation regardless of what they have done. Ever since I was a little kid, I have had a passion to bring restoration to the broken. I can still remember the first time I heard the stories about David's mighty men. I sat wide-eyed at the kitchen table while my dad told me of their amazing exploits. As I sat there that day, my heart pounded in my chest—not at the thought of slaying a thousand men with only my armor bearer (although that is somewhere in a boy's dream), but at the fact that these men who were known as "mighty" were once the outcasts of their society; they were the nobodies, the violators unwanted in their own towns!

That day I was overwhelmed with compassion for the lost. The stories of a few broken men made whole gripped my heart, and somewhere inside of me I decided to dedicate my life to restoring the brokenhearted, even if they themselves were the ones who created the violation.

Each of us, I believe, is a dream that a body has been wrapped around. Beyond our flesh and bones is the DNA of God Himself. His Word says it best: "So God created mankind in his own image . . . male and female he created them." The way God designed life was never meant to be rocket science, nor should it take a book to understand it. But the fortunate thing is, no matter what you have done, where you have been, how high you have climbed or how far you have fallen, there is a road back to wholeness, and today can be your first step.

As you journey your way through this book, I will give you the practical tools to face your innermost fears and find peace in every storm of life, so that you live victorious and win the war within!

God bless,

Jason Vallotton

ONE

Little House on the Prairie

Most people go through life trying not to get hit. We work hard to dodge the punches and avoid conflict, and we even daydream about a "whole new world" instead of learning how to roll with each punch, confront the conflict within and powerfully create a world worth living in. The very way we are born into this world, although traumatic in nature, is a beautiful but graphic picture of life. After a baby spends nine cozy months floating in luxury, something bursts the bubble, and in a moment's time what was baby's paradise changes into a cramping, claustrophobic process of pain and intense, head-squeezing pressure. With a loud scream, each one of us was introduced into a whole new world that way, where, for the first time, we had to work for our oxygen, cry for our food and endure twelve to fifteen months of intense physical therapy in order to take a few clumsy steps.

Right from the start, we face challenges. Yet the idea that trials and troubles are a hazard to the believer conflicts with our God-given purpose of overcoming this world and advancing the Kingdom. In fact, I strongly believe that it is impossible to fulfill the call on our lives without first being willing to face the impossible, learn how to persevere through suffering and become the calm to a raging storm. In Mark 16:17–18, Jesus describes what a believer's life will look like:

> And these signs will accompany those who believe: In my name they will drive out demons; they will speak in new tongues; they will pick up snakes with their hands; and when they drink deadly poison, it will not hurt them at all; they will place their hands on sick people, and they will get well.

Jesus tells us that in His name, every believer will face his or her own fear and will step toward conflict to bring a lasting, powerful solution that will change every atmosphere and create Kingdom culture. This is an incredibly powerful posture to take in life. The challenge in all of this is that you cannot bring change to the outside of whatever you have not confronted on the inside! You can be sure, however, that life is going to test what you truly believe in your core. It certainly has tested me.

My story is one of humble beginnings. I was raised in the little mountain town of Weaverville, California. (Anyone who comes from a place called "Weaverville" has a fair amount of catching up to do in life!) Although I have been known to make fun of my hometown, it was in that town that my heart would learn to love, and it was there that my individuality was formed as I journeyed through adolescence into manhood. Historically, Weaverville was the pot of gold at the end of the rainbow, a place where men tempted fate in pursuit of their dreams. Our town was birthed in the gold rush era. People from all over came to gamble all they had in hopes of striking it rich. Most of these men started with nothing, and most left with nothing except for the invaluable experience life forged into them, a story much like my own.

> You can be sure that life is going to test what you truly believe in your core.

My family is the kind that any kid might wish for. With three other siblings (two older sisters and an older brother), and two incredible, loving parents, there was not a lot left to be desired. I have always likened our family to the one on *Little House on the Prairie*. In all my growing-up years, I can only remember one time when my parents had a heated argument, and even when they had a disagreement, we all knew my dad would apologize for being wrong and it would all be over.

Drama in our house looked like the time when a bear tried to come through our window because my mom had prayed it would come closer. Who does that? Or when my neighbor came unglued because my dog walked on his freshly cleaned concrete with his muddy paws. In all honesty, my neighbor needed some anger management classes like the world needs Jesus. Somehow, he forgot that we lived in "Red-Dirt-Ville, California," where it is impossible to keep concrete clean, no matter how mad you get.

Living in a small town in the mountains has a much simpler feel to it than anywhere else I have ever been. Success looks like a steady job, a few healthy kids and a good church to attend. To be honest, there is something really appealing even to this day about being happy with the small, simple things. Unfortunately, there is not much to do in a place like Weaverville, and because I had no idea (literally) that the rest of the world existed, the only logical conclusion for me after graduating high school was to get married. Why wait? In our family, the men fall in love young. My dad set the trend when he asked my mom to marry him when she was just thirteen years old. Being the opportunist he is, my father felt that there was no need to waste time in fumbling with all of the pointless details that dating can incur. He was set on Mom early, so he sealed the deal then and there!

> To be honest, there is something really appealing even to this day about being happy with the small, simple things.

You know the saying "The apple doesn't fall far from the tree"? It doesn't in my family. I met my girlfriend when I was sixteen, we dated until I graduated and we tied the knot in the summer of 1998. As if that were not enough, we found out two months into our marriage that our first baby was on the way. According to me, I had the beginnings of what was to be my perfect life. Little did I know that my simplistic view of life was about to get much more complicated.

1776

There are so many moments that we live through on this earth, only to forget them the very next day. This moment I am about to describe is not one of those moments. Although I cannot tell you the date and time, I can clearly remember what happened. I began reading a book called *1776*, historian David McCullough's fascinating perspective on the beginning of the Revolutionary War. I would not call myself a book buff, or anything even close to that. Actually, if a book is more than three hundred pages, that is usually enough to deter me from reading it. After briefly picking up this book, however, I could not put it down. The stories of our fearless forefathers, who gave everything they had to gain our freedom as a nation, captured my heart. These men had something worth living for.

Looking back on that time of reading about America's struggle, I was absolutely clueless as to what it was preparing my heart for. I had no idea that in just a few months my whole life was going to fall apart, and I would get the opportunity of a lifetime to deal with the kind of pain that builds character.

So there I was on that fateful day, driving down Benton Street in Redding, California, just thinking to myself, *I want the character of George Washington. . . .* Now if I were smart, I would have stopped my thoughts right there. But for some reason, I did what no one should ever do if he or she has not counted the cost: I moved that idea from my brain to my lips. Before I could stop myself, I said to the Lord out loud, "I want the character of George Washington."

> The stories of our fearless forefathers, who gave everything they had to gain our freedom as a nation, captured my heart.

I am not sure exactly why it always happens this way, but it does. You can pray a thousand prayers, but it seems as though the one the Lord decides to answer is the one you then think maybe you *never* should have prayed (probably the one having something to do with building character).

If I had thought about it a little bit longer, I would have realized what I was asking. George Washington was not a man who lived an untested life. He wrote a letter to a family member in 1755, during the French and Indian War, saying that he had escaped uninjured, but that "I had four bullets through my coat, and two horses shot under me." It is said of George that he believed he could not die until his "appointed time," so he would undertake these crazy feats of valor against all odds, with little or no fear. And here I was, praying that I would have character like his.

As the Bible says, "Ask and it will be given to you" (Luke 11:9). I was asking, and I did receive! I am not sure if you have ever shared a similar experience, but in about four months' time, my life was completely set on fire. Everything that had been stable soon began to shake. This process began when a very close family member went through a horrific nervous breakdown. I spent countless hours in prayer and on the phone, contending for breakthrough and believing that peace was just around the corner. I had done a lot of counseling in my job, and I had helped people through these types of issues before. But two months later, another family member suffered a similar attack.

What's going on? I asked myself. This whole process had started in October 2007, and now it was December. Sometimes I am not the most spiritually "in tune" person, but even I could tell that "hell had come to breakfast." My hopes were that this visit was just one meal. Unfortunately, it was only the beginning of what would take almost two years to walk through.

When the Temperature Dropped

So there I was, literally in the middle of winter, but I was also slowly beginning to feel colder inside than I had ever felt before. I had never had one close family member go through something like this, let alone two at the same time. As the days passed, I realized there was not going to be a quick fix. Their dark nights of the soul had seemingly come to stay.

There is no feeling quite like that of being a powerless bystander to a total disaster. Watching your loved ones, day in and day out, tremble under the thought of having to face another morning does something to a man's soul. Momentum is a force to be reckoned with. Once the train gets going, it is a bear to stop, and things were about to get worse. February rolled around, and it had been four months since the beginning of it all. I welcomed the new month with open arms.

> Our family is the type that carries each other's burdens, sometimes to a fault.

I was hoping for crisp morning air and freedom from those long, dark nights that had been such a constant weight on me, since our family is the type that carries each other's burdens, sometimes to a fault.

As the new month began to unfold, it was not long before I started to realize that I was feeling more alone at home than usual. One thing you need to understand is that feeling alone in my house was almost an impossibility back then. I had three kids: Evan, my youngest, was three at the time; Rilie, my princess, was six; and Elijah, my oldest, was eight. And of course there was my wife, to whom I had been married for nine years. Alone time at my house existed only between the hours of 12:00 a.m. and 6:00 a.m., if I was lucky. The other eighteen hours were spent filling sippy cups, playing WWE (World Wrestling Entertainment) in the living room and tending to every need ever known to man (or child). There was never a dull moment around my house. My "alone at home" feeling was not being produced by the absence of people, however, but rather by the absence of connection in my marriage.

At first, I was not all that concerned about my emotional state of being. This was not the first time I had felt lonely in my house, and I was sure it was not going to be the last. If you have been married for any significant amount of time, you know loneliness is not a freak incident, but rather a season you sometimes go through as lovers.

There were so many contributing factors feeding into the feelings I had going on inside. On my end of the deal, I felt a lot of pressure due to what my extended family was going through, and it was threatening my overall sense of peace. Plus, I was the father of three very energetic kids. So there we were, going through one of those times when you need the commitment part of love to kick in and pull you close.

After about a week of feeling lonely, however, I realized it was not going to go away on its own. I felt as if my wife and I were magnets that had somehow gotten flipped around, and connecting had become an impossible feat. At this point, I knew I was in over my head and in need of intervention.

As time passed, it was looking as though my love for my wife was not going to be enough. For so long, our simple connection was all that we had needed, but now neither any amount of counseling nor my best efforts were enough to satisfy her. In a matter of months, my life had completely turned to ash. My marriage was over, and it was now time to face reality or tuck tail and run!

All throughout that time when I was reading *1776*, I used to think to myself how lucky a person like George Washington was, not because he did not die in battle or because he made the history books, but because he had a battle to fight. He had an opportunity to test his mettle and fill himself with enough courage so that death no longer held its sting.

They say that heroes are found on the battlefield, and if what they say is true, I now had my opportunity to show the kind of character I admired in George Washington.

Lessons from the Past

Unfortunately, my story is not unique. The older I become, the more I realize how great the war is we are in, and how ill-equipped we are. I spent twelve years in school learning (at least, that's what I was trying to do). I was a horrible student. For me, sitting in one place for an extended period of time was literally torture. Add to that a touch of ADD, little or no academic skill and a private school with horrible funding. Basically, I had no chance of making the grade.

I now know what we all know—making good grades in school can be almost irrelevant to being successful in navigating the life issues we all face on a regular basis. As a counselor, I ask my clients all the time, "Who taught you to communicate?" "What is your process for dealing with pain?" "Do you know what your red flags and triggers are?" Even the most scholastically educated people either somehow managed to skip the courses dealing with this stuff, or those courses don't exist!

To add fuel to an already raging fire in me, when our parents grew up they had been in the same predicament as we were, or worse. Their parents were literally fighting on actual battlefields, or suffering through the Great Depression, or stuck in an oppressive culture that suppressed people's feelings and praised outward control. Then they all passed down to us some of their inability to deal with certain life issues, and the effects multiplied. Now as a result, we live in a society in which many people have lost their moral compass and are completely out of control, mostly due to being ill-equipped to face life.

> It is our inner world that dictates the culture we create, no matter the issue.

Let's be honest, no one dreams of burning out at work, having a failing marriage or raising kids who cannot stand spending time at home. Logically, we know that we judge ourselves against some picture-perfect Instagram world in our heads, and that when we don't measure up, our demeaning self-talk is toxic to the soul. But where else do we start, and what do we do?

I spent two years walking out of my prison of pain and into wholeness. As you can imagine, I was terrified at first. There were so many unanswered questions, and only a few teachers to run to. Now, over a decade later, I have seen the fruit that has come out of those years in my life, and the invaluable tools that I gained along the way. It is so easy to focus on what is happening on the outside, or on the particulars of each circumstance. It is our inner world, however, that dictates the culture we create, no matter the issue.

Regardless of whether your story is mine or not, the practical concepts I have learned and have used to shape my life into what it is today are what I want to give to you. In the next several chapters, I want to talk with you about how to place God at the center of your life, confront your fears and walk practically out of pain into a place of real peace and hope. Together, we will win the war within!

REFLECT

1. Reflecting on your life, are there any punches you are trying to dodge, conflicts you are trying to avoid on the outside or conflicts you need to address within?

2. If you answered yes to any part of question 1 (or more than one part), who is going to be on your team to help you find breakthrough in these areas? It may be helpful to find a life coach, counselor or pastor who has the skills necessary to help you.

3. What fruits are you hoping to discover in your life once you learn to process what you have been avoiding?

4. What kind of character traits are you hoping to build as you fight and win the war within?

TWO

God Spot

We all have our "demons" in life. I know you cringe at that word, but it's true. For so many of us, life gets molded around what we are willing to face, and we are confined to our little boxes of safety, protected from the outside world. Fear draws the boundary lines, and the playing field inside is our comfort. It is so easy to let the unknown decide how far to go and what we will become. For most people, life becomes about safety and comfort. Our subconscious takes over, and before we know it autopilot kicks in and we are just going through the motions of a mediocre life. We call this living the good life, but in reality, we are boxed in by fear and are unable to really live. Instead, we are merely surviving.

Psychologists say that our number one drive as human beings is our instinct to survive. Above everything else, this Neanderthalian impulse is literally how humans have beaten the odds for thousands of years. Our ability to analyze a situation and predict danger is crucial to our well-being and longevity. Yet as Bob Dylan put it in his famous song title, "The Times They Are a-Changin'," while we are still hiding in our caves with spears in hand, ready to take on the hypothetical sabertooth. Honestly, it is hard to blame anyone when you take a look at the world most people grow up in. More than 20 million children in the United States live in a home without the physical presence of a father. Millions more have dads who are physically present, but emotionally absent. If it were classified as a disease, fatherlessness would be an epidemic worthy of attention as a national emergency. Furthermore, if you look at the statistics on what happens when there is no father present, they are staggering. Kids have to grow up faster, deal with life issues with no real guidance and often suffer the trauma of living in constant abuse. And this is just one issue that plagues us.

> When we build a culture where fear is a friend that becomes our protector, we are bound by the wrong master.

The problem is not that people have to move in and out of survival mode for different seasons of life. After all, survival is essential. When we build a culture where fear is a friend that becomes our protector, however, we are bound by the wrong master.

My dad used to tell me, "There is almost always some truth inside each lie." This is where most people get caught. When you really understand how a culture of fear is built, it is shocking how much truth is built into it. The little boy who learns not to express any of his needs at home because he is constantly fed rejection and insult as a result figures he might be better off to stay silent than be punished. Or there is the child who learns how to use anger to fight because he is constantly bullied.

As adults, these same people no longer need what kept them safe as children, but because they are convinced unconsciously that their partnership with fear is essential, what once kept them alive through fear will remain and will eventually destroy their life. Fear takes root at such a young age that we are often unaware of what is actually happening until it is too late. And often, as adults we buy in to the beliefs that have been scored into our fragile young minds—beliefs about who we are and what we need to do to survive.

Left Behind

My parents believed strongly in giving us kids the best foundation possible. This meant that my siblings and I attended our local Christian school instead of a public school. For my parents, this was an incredible sacrifice. Back when I was a boy, we basically lived paycheck to paycheck. "Robbing from Peter to pay Paul" is how my mom would put it. There was barely enough money most of the time, and sometimes not enough. Despite the financial hardship, however, my parents were bound and determined to carry the extra burden of paying for a private school if it meant we would be better off for it.

Small-town Christian school had its benefits, but also sometimes its major downsides, especially in the 1980s! For starters, spankings were handed out on the regular at school. Yup, you read that right. Act out in class and there was no need for your parents to come deal with it. Our principal would take care of it himself, plus you knew that when Dad found out about it, you were going to get round two on the backside. As funny as this is to me now, looking back I can see how traumatic it was for some of the kids. I am not anti-spanking by any means, but being spanked by a virtual stranger at school was a bit much.

The absolute worst, most nightmarish day I have ever had in class, however, was when our whole school had to watch the movie *A Thief in the Night*. If you have never seen the film, it is basically a dramatized version of what people think will happen if we all get raptured. Well, at least if most of us get raptured . . .

As far as I can remember, the movie starts out with normal families playing in a theme park, enjoying life and casually talking about accepting Jesus into their hearts. As a kid, I remember being stoked about being able to watch a show during class time—when all of a sudden the plot thickened. People start disappearing from the earth as if they were the targets of some kind of alien abduction. The guy who was mowing the lawn vanishes, planes fall out of the sky, kids are left frantically searching for their parents as pots of food boil over on the stove. As if that were not bad enough, into the plot walks the "mark of the beast."

By the end of that film, I was completely terrified. It scared the "hell" right into me. I accepted fear as my lord and savior and gave Jesus my heart—or what was left of it. I literally spent months terrified that I was going to wake up and no one was going to be home except for me, scared out of my mind and left behind!

> I accepted fear as my lord and savior and gave Jesus my heart—or what was left of it.

My childhood was riddled with fear. I regularly sneaked into my parents' bedroom at night and slept on their floor, as it was often the only place I could fall asleep. I had an irrational fear of dying, along with nightmares and a deep knowing that at some point, I was probably going to be left here on this earth alone.

At around the age of fourteen, I hit an all-time low. I remember weeks where I would get dropped off at home after school in the wintertime and no one would be home. I was absolutely terrified as my mind raced through the possibilities of a child abduction taking place, or the threat of robbers breaking into our house, only to find me all by myself. Each day, I would go upstairs to my room, load my 12-gauge shotgun and sit on the couch, petrified, until my family came home. My parents could not leave the house without my knowing where they were going, and often I would interrupt their time with friends to have them come home early.

After months of complete torment, it was apparent that this was not going to leave on its own and something needed to change. For the first time in my life, I began to learn how to take my thoughts captive. My dad taught me that not all my thoughts are my own, that we have an enemy, and that I am not powerless over him. To this day, I still use a tool he taught me about. When a thought tries to come into my mind, I close my eyes and imagine an impenetrable wall shielding me from it. Then come the incinerators that burn up the lie. Before you know it, what was once a scary, make-believe world is merely dust. . . .

My parents worked hard to be present in that season when I was fearful constantly. They taught me how to pray, introduced me to the Holy Spirit and His peace and ultimately walked me through the scariest time in my life. But what I did not realize as a kid was that the very thing that had gotten me saved was keeping me from living free. When I watched that movie in grade school, I really was terrified. I really did want to give my heart to Jesus so that I would not be left on this scorched earth. Although my motives were not evil, they were all deeply rooted in fear.

First John 4:18 says, "There is no fear in love. But perfect love drives out fear." As a young man, I had it all wrong and did not even know it. I had given my life to the Lord, but because fear was my motivating factor, as soon as fear was gone, so was I. In fact, it is almost impossible to stay close to the God of love when you are full of the thing that love casts out. Whatever you fear will ultimately become your master. This is the process of allowing deception to take control of your mind. It all starts by allowing small, cunning lies to creep in undetected. At first, they seem rational—a vital contribution to the well-being of your personhood. They come cloaked in common sense and take up residence inside logic and reason. But their deception is deep and destructive. Their words have nothing to do with the Father's heart, for they are only a façade of true light.

> It is almost impossible to stay close to the God of love when you are full of the thing that love casts out.

Entire identities and worldviews can be founded on lies. Obviously, this is catastrophic to the health and well-being of the individuals who do so. Such lies should be addressed immediately and undone in order to remove the stronghold of fear. Yet to overpower these destructive lies, we must first recognize them as lies. And because we are often oblivious to what is going on inside us, it can be hard to recognize what is actually driving us.

Who or What Is in Your "God Spot"?

I spent years in my marriage scared to express needs, not wanting to "rock the boat," and I did not even know it. My high pleaser personality blinded me to the fact that I had put my wife in my God spot. On the outside, it looked as if I were the brave husband who was laying his life down like Jesus, but on the inside, I was terrified of conflict.

Winning this war within starts by disempowering fear and placing God back into the center of our life. Psalm 23 (NASB) paints an amazing picture of what it looks like to have God as the main source of our life, leading us out of the shadow of death:

> The LORD is my shepherd,
> I shall not want.
> He makes me lie down in green pastures;
> He leads me beside quiet waters.
> He restores my soul;
> He guides me in the paths of righteousness
> For His name's sake.
>
> Even though I walk through the valley of the
> shadow of death,
> I fear no evil, for You are with me;
> Your rod and Your staff, they comfort me.
> You prepare a table before me in the presence of
> my enemies;
> You have anointed my head with oil;
> My cup overflows.
> Surely goodness and lovingkindness will follow
> me all the days of my life,
> And I will dwell in the house of the Lord forever.

These few verses are a powerful revelation of what happens to us when God is our master and main source of strength. Not only are we led to a place of quiet rest, but we are also restored in that place.

The beautiful part of this passage is that it covers all of life, and even death. David says, "Even though I walk through the valley of the shadow of death, I fear no evil, for You are with me; Your rod and Your staff, they comfort me" (verse 4). I want you to notice that he did not say that God is his Shepherd because He bails him out of bad situations. Rather, God is the director and the source of his life in every circumstance.

> Winning this war within starts by disempowering fear and placing God back into the center of our life.

God is the Shepherd of our lives, even when we walk through the valley of the shadow of death. The peace of God therefore wraps around us while He leads the way. One of the best ways we can find out who is leading us is to stop and take a look at our everyday life. What has become our main source of direction, protection, comfort, healing, unconditional love and identity? Where do we go on a daily basis to get our needs met? Ask yourself those questions. Your answers will reveal a lot about *who* or *what* is in your "God spot."

The danger here is that it is so easy to think that God is in control of our life when it is sunny out and the daisies are in full bloom. Success can skew our view, causing us to believe we have something that we really don't. Wall Street's history supports that. Whenever the stock market has plummeted, the pillars of clay that once felt so secure beneath people's feet crumble to the ground, leaving seemingly successful people in despair. When the scales of success fall off our eyes, stark reality begins to set in. The positive side of it is that in these circumstances, many people cry out to God.

Just because we cry out to God in desperate times, however, does not mean He is the center of our universe. Actually, many times I have found the opposite is true in most people's lives. Take 9/11, for example. When the Twin Towers came crumbling to the ground, the crushing blow dropped America to its knees. People were literally shaken to their core, and they cried out in desperation for God to help them. For a few weeks, it felt as if the world slowed down and people from all over our nation began to get right with the Lord out of fear that everything was coming to an end. Thousands of people flooded the altars of our churches, but it did not take long for the shock to wear off and life to return to "normal"—without God.

Putting God Back in Control

We were never created to be a powerless people, subject to the happiness or depression of the environment around us. Rather, our source of wholeness is derived from the Author Himself. God is the only one who can offer us love and security, regardless of our circumstances.

Placing God on the throne of our lives is not rocket science, but it does require diligence and taking the right steps. There are four steps I have identified that will take you in the right direction toward putting God back in control of your life—steps I followed myself when I put Him back in the "God spot" in my life. They are (1) do the work of repentance, (2) start the messy cleanup, (3) think differently

> God is the only one who can offer us love and security, regardless of our circumstances.

and (4) set healthy boundaries. Let's look at each of these steps in a little more detail.

First Step: Do the Work of Repentance

The very first step to reestablishing God on the throne of your life is repentance. The original Greek word for repent is *metanoeo*, which means to change the way you think. Repentance roots out inferior and faulty thought processes and replaces them with truth. It is not only necessary to repent for removing God out of His rightful spot in our lives, but we also need to repent for the reasons *why* we displaced Him.

It is so important for us to get to the root issues that have caused the faulty thinking in our hearts. This is where most people miss the bus. They are genuinely sorry for their actions, but because they have no idea what is driving them (what the root issue is), they cannot keep their actions and heart in line with their convictions. They therefore return once again to their old cycle of thinking.

When I realized that I had put my wife in my "God spot," I had to go back and figure out *why* I had chosen to do that, and then I could truly repent.

Second Step: Start the Messy Cleanup

After repentance (changing the way we think), we often have to go back and clean up our mess. Many of us have a huge misconception about what cleaning up our mess really looks like. We have been taught through our childhood experiences that the word *sorry* fixes everything. This could not be further from the truth. Saying "I'm sorry" does not fix anything. I know this because I have three kids! On any given day, it is only a matter of time before one of my children acts out in a "not so fun way" toward one of his or her siblings. Usually, it is some sort of short-lived, spur-of-the-moment flare-up about who is going to get the middle seat in the car or who is going to consume the coveted last Go-Gurt in the freezer. Kids can always find something to argue about.

It is tempting as a parent to stop the argument as quickly as possible while exerting the least amount of effort, the goal being to restore chaos to a manageable level. In our efforts to restore order, it is really easy to say something like this: "Kids, knock it off! Elijah, tell your sister you're sorry for being rude to her, or you can go spend the rest of the day in your room!"

Now, I am as guilty as anybody else when it comes to statements like that. The problem with just telling my kids what to do and what to say, however, is that then the change is not really coming from their own hearts. Any apology they offer is never genuine enough to change their behavior, so the problem still exists.

If our kids are going to change their behavior, they need to be able to figure out why they chose to be disrespectful, and then they must want to choose a different behavior so that their "sorry" is productive.

It is no different for you and me. The goal of repentance is not simply to say the words "I'm sorry," but rather to find the root of the issue so we can fix the behavior.

Third Step: Think Differently

A lot of situations in life seem hard to overcome because of the level of bravery it takes to actually acknowledge that there is a problem. We have all met people with the proverbial pet elephant standing in their living room. These people are oblivious to the elephant—their internal world—but usually are quick to point out the elephant standing in other people's living rooms.

To change the metaphor a bit, these people are victims turned vampires. The victim mentality is one of the deadliest mindsets, because a victim is totally incapable of changing his or her environment. Victims spend massive amounts of time sucking the life out of everyone else, because they live in a powerless state of mind. Victims believe that their external world has to change in order for them to be okay. Because a victim is so out of control internally, he or she feels an enormous need to control everyone else.

Powerlessness is the process of giving away ownership and empowering someone or something else as your sole decision maker. You cannot fix something for which you are unwilling to take ownership. It is simply impossible. Taking ownership for your decisions and your problems is the only way to ever become a healthy person. Regardless of what you have come to believe, you are responsible for your own life and actions. When you give up that right to someone else, you render yourself powerless.

Recently, I counseled a couple who typified the victim mentality. Their cry for help came in the form of a Facebook chat. I sat down with my friend Jim and began to assess what was going on. It did not take him long to explain to me that his wife, Sarah, was impossible to please. He said she was a black hole that nothing could ever fill, and worse yet, she was a nag. She had no respect for his boundaries, especially when their discussions morphed into arguments. This usually resulted in Jim punching holes in the wall or smashing things.

"She won't let me leave the room or give me time to think; she just keeps hounding me," Jim complained. "Sarah totally controls me!"

My first thought was, *Wowza! I'm so glad I'm not in this guy's shoes!* After giving him time to talk and vent, I began to ask him some pointed questions about himself. First, I asked what he had done to work on his relationship with his wife.

There was a long pause, accompanied by a sigh. "Um, I guess I'm here," he said.

"Okay," I said. "Did you set up this meeting, or did Sarah?" (I already knew the answer to this question, but I really wanted Jim to know the answer for himself.)

"Uh, she did," he admitted.

Continuing on that train of thought, I said, "Whom have you gone to in order to get some help with your relationship?"

Thinking for a second, Jim responded, "Well, I talk to my mom sometimes. Actually, my mom found out about our marital problems because Sarah called her. She normally calls my parents when we are hard at it."

At this point, I was starting to see a pattern in Jim's life. As the questions continued, I found out that Jim did not talk to anyone about his marriage, including his best friend. To make matters worse, when I asked him what he did to get rid of his pain and frustration, his response was, "I normally just try to forget about it."

It would not take a psychiatrist to figure out that Jim's plan of ignoring his frustration and stuffing his pain was not working. This man was punching holes in the wall and turning over tables in their house, but that kind of approach obviously was never going to solve anything.

"Jim, it doesn't seem as if your plan has been working very well," I said. "What have you done to meet your wife's needs in her love languages?" (I was referring to Dr. Gary Chapman's research on the five primary ways people express and interpret love, which are words of affirmation, quality time, receiving gifts, acts of service and physical touch. You can find out more about the five love languages from Dr. Chapman's books or from visiting www.5lovelanguages.com.)

Annoyed, Jim replied, "Even if I try, I don't ever seem to be able to meet them. I've felt really frustrated lately trying to meet Sarah's needs. It feels pretty hopeless."

You could hear in Jim's tone of voice the irritation he was carrying inside. I asked him, "Jim, what are you going to do about your marriage?"

"I don't know. I wish Sarah wasn't such a mess and wasn't so hard to live with," he said.

It was time for me to give some feedback. "Jim, it doesn't feel as if she's really the whole problem. You've made her responsible for getting help for you guys. She's the one who's contacting your parents and me. You haven't done anything proactive to work on your relationship, other than the things she hounds you about, and you have no process for dealing with the pain and frustration you feel from not being successful. And finally, you still believe that she's the sole problem. I'm not surprised that she nags you, Jim. It's the only way that you've ever become motivated in this relationship. You've empowered her to be your mother."

I could see the lightbulb exploding in his brain. For the first time in a long while, Jim was beginning to realize that he had given his power away to his wife. She had become responsible for the health of their relationship. As long as he kept hanging on to this belief system, he would always be powerless to fix what was going on inside him.

So many people are like Jim. They create a belief system that tells them they are not responsible for the condition of their life. It is less painful to believe that their problems are everyone else's fault. When I first talked with Jim, he had given up on his marriage relationship. He told his wife that he was considering getting a divorce because she was making him miserable. What Jim did not realize was that if he spent less time worrying about what Sarah was going to do and more time trying to figure out what he was going to do, he could actually fix the majority of his problems. But Jim had never taken personal responsibility for his life and marriage, so he was always frustrated and overwhelmed because his peace and happiness were at the mercy of his wife.

Once Jim realized he had given all his power away, he was then able to repent for his victim mentality and figure out what he was going to do to get his power back and start loving his wife. Today, Jim is no longer a victim, and his marriage is flourishing.

I have always said that anytime a problem is 100 percent my fault, it's a good day! I can fix anything that is my fault, but I cannot fix anything I don't control. The day that you take ownership for your life is the day that you begin to take control again. Being powerful does not mean putting yourself in the "God spot." It means being able to choose for yourself who occupies that spot in your life. By taking ownership, you can put God in His rightful place, not yourself or another person.

Fourth Step: Set Healthy Boundaries

One of the major aspects of being in control of your life is having the ability to set healthy boundaries with people. Proverbs 25:28 says, "Like a city whose walls are broken through is a person who lacks self-control." The person who lacks the ability to set boundaries will end up being like a broken-down, pillaged city. A defenseless city gets plundered and has nothing of value left to offer anyone.

Personal boundaries are like the protective walls of an ancient city. The purpose of having good boundaries is to protect and nourish yourself so you can cultivate healthy relationships with others. Without the ability to protect yourself, you have no way to provide protection for anyone else in your life.

> The purpose of having good boundaries is to protect and nourish yourself so you can cultivate healthy relationships with others.

A person establishes healthy boundaries through the process of defining his or her virtues, values and needs, and then communicating those to the people he or she is in relationship with. When you articulate your boundaries to people, they have the opportunity to respect your needs and virtues and protect your relationship with them. And when they value and protect the things that are important to you, the relationship between you flourishes. This is the process that builds trust between you and others.

Another great aspect of boundaries is the ability to let people know what you can do/will do and can't do/won't do. You actually have the right and the ability to set limits with others for the health of the relationship. There are no healthy relationships without healthy boundaries.

One of the things we all need to keep in mind when we are setting boundaries is that the primary goal should be to build stronger and deeper relationships with people. Yes, boundaries do keep some people out of relationship with us when they refuse to respect those boundaries. But the main goal of telling people what we need and feel is so that they can do the things that cultivate a healthy relationship with us, not so that we have a valid reason to scratch them off our friend list.

Powerful people know what they need and what they are going to do. They are able to set boundaries, because they believe that no one else is responsible for them. No matter what the situation, they are still able to be powerful and choose their responses, because no one else but God is in control of their future. When I understood this truth as it related to my wife, it was a turning point in my ability to approach the future with peace. But I still needed to get free from my sense of the injustice of it all. In the next chapter, we will look more closely at how justice is served.

REFLECT

1. Who or what is in the "God spot" of your life? You will know it is not God if you are feeling anxiety about areas only He should be in control of. When we have God in His rightful spot, our anxiety level drops.

2. In order to put God back in your God spot, you need to know what is at the root of that displacement. If God is not in your God spot, do you know why you have displaced Him? (Refer back to this chapter's section "Who or What Is in Your God Spot?" to make sure you understand the concept of getting to the root.)

3. Take some time to ask yourself and God, *What would it look like for me to take ownership in my repentance process?* Taking ownership may include processing with a friend or going to see a counselor. Note that it is important to find practical, everyday steps you can take to create new habits and break unhealthy cycles in your life.

4. When you don't feel like doing the work of daily repentance, what will you do to motivate yourself or to stay accountable? (It is helpful to create small goals as you go along that lead you to success.) For example, if I know I have put someone other than God in my God spot and my relationship with that person is unhealthy, I will take a month to work

on it. I make it my goal to read and understand the book *Boundaries* by Dr. Henry Cloud and Dr. John Townsend (Zondervan, 2017) the first two weeks, and then the third and fourth weeks I will work with a friend and/or counselor to help me set the correct boundaries. From there, I will continue to work on understanding why I put that person in the place of God, and I will uproot the faulty belief system behind it and get my needs met in a healthy way.

THREE

Justice Served

The day my wife walked out the door of my life, I experienced everything through a haze. Inside, my bleeding heart was crying out for justice. After all, it was not as if I were the only one carrying the pain of her loss. My children's hearts had been shattered into a thousand tiny pieces in the process. Words don't bring any real solace to kids who are watching the deconstruction of a family.

What we often forget is that the compounding consequences of such a situation affect more than just us. More often than not, the people who suffer even more are those who have little or no responsibility in the matter, especially those we love the most. My kids were no exception. For me, it was easy to imagine myself being able to walk away from this disaster, never having to see or hear from my ex-wife ever again. But the reality was, I was going to spend the rest of my life raising kids with the person who had hurt me the most. And I was going to have to share my kids with whomever she chose. To me, it seemed as though there was nothing more unjust in this world than the betrayal of a marriage.

A Change of Heart

As the days passed, my soul was at war within itself. I was torn between my feelings of anger and what I had been taught my whole life about forgiveness. The problem was, I needed justice. I began to think and write about what true justice is. I knew that whatever it was, I had to have it for myself and for my kids. My soul ached at the thought of what my children were going through, along with the fact that they did not deserve this, and neither did I. As I started to pursue the truth, I began to realize that justice is much different than what my instincts were telling me.

> As I started to pursue the truth, I began to realize that justice is much different than what my instincts were telling me.

I often envisioned myself like a cowboy in an Old West showdown, doling out justice with a six-shooter. There were so many days when I wanted to do whatever it took to get even, yet I knew that two wrongs would never equal a right. Furthermore, if I punished my ex-wife to take revenge, my actions would be just as selfish as hers. My kids would ultimately be the ones who would suffer the most from my destructive behavior. What I really needed was a solution that would make this whole situation better. I did not need to pour gasoline on this already raging fire.

My entire world seemed to be hanging in the balance that hinged on the answers to two questions: *What is true justice? How do I get it?* I began to think about my own failures. I lay awake deep into the night, pondering on how my decisions had cost a Man His life. It was not something I had ever planned, nor would I ever make some of those poor decisions on purpose again. But the fact is that it was my sin that drove the nails through Jesus' flesh, and it was my selfishness that pierced His side. If that were not enough, it was my need for acceptance that broke open His back with the Roman whip.

We are all guilty of His murder, each and every one of us. Because of our inability to live a sinless life, God gave up His only Son to pay for our foolishness and inability to live right. God originally set up the world so that we could have an amazing relationship with Him. He created us to be His sons and daughters, and He wants us to live eternally with Him. The only thing that could ever separate us from our rightful place with God is sin. Sin is our archenemy because it devastates our lives and destroys our relationship with God.

Isaiah paints a beautiful picture of what Christ went through to forgive our sins and reconcile us to God:

Who believes what we've heard and seen? Who would have thought God's saving power would look like this?

The servant grew up before God—a scrawny seedling, a scrubby plant in a parched field. There was nothing attractive about him, nothing to cause us to take a second look. He was looked down on and passed over, a man who suffered, who knew pain firsthand. One look at him and people turned away. We looked down on him, thought he was scum. But the fact is, it was *our* pains he carried—*our* disfigurements, all the things wrong with *us*. We thought he brought it on himself, that God was punishing him for his own failures. But it was our sins that did that to him, that ripped and tore and crushed him—*our sins!* He took the punishment, and that made us whole. Through his bruises we get healed. We're all like sheep who've wandered off and gotten lost. We've all done our own thing, gone our own way. And God has piled all our sins, everything we've done wrong, on him, on him.

He was beaten, he was tortured, but he didn't say a word. Like a lamb taken to be slaughtered and like a sheep being sheared, he took it all in silence. Justice miscarried, and he was led off—and did anyone really know what was happening? He died without a thought for his own welfare, beaten bloody for the sins of my people. They buried him with the wicked, threw him in a grave with a rich man, even though he'd never hurt a soul or said one word that wasn't true.

Still, it's what God had in mind all along, to crush him with pain. The plan was that he give himself as an offering for sin so that he'd see life come from it—life, life, and more life. And God's plan will deeply prosper through him.

Out of that terrible travail of soul, he'll see that it's worth it and be glad he did it. Through what he experienced, my righteous one, my servant, will make many "righteous ones," as he himself carries the burden of their sins. Therefore I'll reward him extravagantly—the best of everything, the highest honors—because he looked death in the face and didn't flinch, because he embraced the company of the lowest. He took on his own shoulders the sin of the many, he took up the cause of all the black sheep.

Isaiah 53:1–12 MESSAGE

The day Jesus was crushed for our sins, He revealed the meaning of true justice. Justice was no longer found in revenge, but in forgiveness. Jesus died so that we could be forgiven. Unforgiveness therefore became an injustice, because lack of forgiveness nullifies the payment Christ made for us with His own blood.

There really is no justice in a broken life! This revelation rocked me to the core as I began to change the way I saw my circumstances. When I was in need of forgiveness, Jesus gave it to me. For the first time,

> The day Jesus was crushed for our sins, He revealed the meaning of true justice.

I realized that the only way I was ever going to get justice in this relationship was to pray that my ex-wife would get what Jesus paid for. And the only way that my kids were going to win in this mess was to have their mom become a whole person. Once I realized the truth, the urge to punish her for her actions began to fade away. I stopped lying awake at night thinking of ways she could be punished, and I began contending for her health and well-being.

Now, That's Justice

Over the years, I have worked with literally hundreds of people who have been victims of some sort of violation. In my line of work, it is not uncommon on a weekly basis for me to help someone who has been raped, cheated on, verbally abused, lied to, or all of the above. As you can probably imagine, experiencing any one of these things can be terribly damaging. But the most damaging aspect of being violated is when the person who was hurt moves into the role of the "punisher" in search of justice.

The "punisher" is a hard-hearted taskmaster fueled by bitterness and anger. His or her destructive actions are self-justified by an overwhelming sense of injustice and a need for recompense. Although the punisher person is not inherently evil, he or she has been deceived into believing that somehow the fruit of taking revenge is going to be peace.

I know this next truth is a hard pill to swallow, especially if you have been wronged, but here it is: Regardless of why you have made bitterness and hatred your best friends, if you carry them around long enough, they will eventually eat you from the inside out.

If you attended Sunday school as a child, you will probably remember the parable recorded in Matthew 18:21–35 of the unforgiving servant. In this parable, Jesus explains this principle of forgiveness, and the lack of it. He tells of a king who wanted to reconcile his accounts with his servants. One servant brought before the king owed him way more than he could ever pay back. When the king realized this, he commanded that the servant, his wife and his kids be sold for payment. When the servant heard this, he threw himself to his knees and begged for mercy, saying, "Lord, have patience with me and I'll repay you all!" In that moment, the king was so moved with compassion that he forgave this servant all his debt.

> Regardless of why you have made bitterness and hatred your best friends, if you carry them around long enough, they will eventually eat you from the inside out.

Not long afterward, this same servant went out and found one of his fellow servants who owed him just a few dollars. He grabbed the man by the throat and demanded, "Pay me what you owe!"

His fellow servant fell down at his feet and begged, "Have patience with me, and I will repay you!"

The first servant would not show any mercy, and he had the man cast into prison. When their fellow servants saw what he had done, they came and told their master everything.

Angrily, the king called the first servant back in. "You wicked servant!" he said. "I forgave you all that debt, because you begged me to do so. Shouldn't you also have had mercy on your fellow servant, even as I had mercy on you?" Then he turned the servant over to the jailers to be tortured until he could pay all that he owed.

Don't you wish the parable would end there? But Jesus throws in one last little line that makes this whole story so pertinent: "This is how my heavenly Father will treat each of you unless you forgive your brother or sister from your heart" (Matthew 18:35).

The principle in this parable is profoundly simple: When you have been forgiven more than you could ever possibly repay, you are expected to forgive in the same fashion. In the event that you forget what was so selflessly given to you, your selfishness will find a home for you in the arms of the tormentors.

Because of what Christ did for us on the cross, and because of the ministry we have been given—to let Him live His nature through us so that others will be drawn to Him, or as Scripture says, "be reconciled" to Him—there is no way that you and I can operate as "punishers" and live in the Kingdom of God. It just doesn't work!

Paul teaches us in 2 Corinthians 5:17 that we are *new creations* in Christ. He goes on to explain that God reconciled us to Himself by not counting our sins against us, and then he reminds us that we have been given the ministry of reconciliation (see verse 19). When you break this passage down, you begin to realize that our ministry as believers in Christ is not to convince the world of their sin. Rather, we are to help reconcile the world back to Christ by not holding people's sins against them. The justice that we need when we have been wronged will be given to us as we help reconcile the world to Jesus.

1. Honestly identify whether or not you are harboring any bitterness and/or hatred. If you are, does your view of justice line up with God's view? What needs to change to bring you into alignment with His view?

2. Why doesn't it work to become a "punisher" in the Kingdom of God? What is the alternative?

3. Is there an area in your life where you have been seeking justice? Regardless of how you feel, take some time each day to ask God what true justice looks like for your situation. Write down what He says and meditate on it until you believe it.

4. In view of the payment Christ made for us with His own blood, in what way does unforgiveness become an injustice? (In chapter 7, I will walk you more fully through the forgiveness process.)

FOUR

The Fruit of Hard Times

So often, the beautiful things of life are hidden just beyond our breaking point. The fact that you are reading this book tells me that you probably understand some of what I am talking about. There is a blessing for us when we press through hard times, because the road to wholeness leads down the path of perseverance. It is crucial to have the right mindset in trying times so that we can emerge victorious on the other side of the trials.

Our culture's expectation of instant gratification in this information age has robbed us of the understanding of the blessings of perseverance and the lessons of sowing and reaping. Let's focus for a few pages on the two vastly different viewpoints of life that represent either the path to a blessed future or the path to always struggling to find a better day. Let's also see if we can unearth the treasures that are so necessary to wholeness and blessing in our personal lives. The principles in this chapter are what helped me get past my painful situation of our family breakup and receive the promise that trials are supposed to yield.

Consider the Farmer

The pain of plowing! But, oh, the reward of reaping! Broken blisters cover the farmer's hands as he works to break up the heat-baked ground. Beaten down by the scorching sun, he can find no escape from the hot, dusty air that his labor is producing. He works tirelessly from dawn till dusk, day in and day out, to produce something that he won't be able to enjoy for months to come. The work is endlessly grueling. For him, breaking the hard ground is only the first part in this long process of sowing seed.

It is the fruit of the hard times that will carry the farmer through the good times. The fruit he produces in his toils will actually create the enjoyable seasons of his near future. The farmer understands this principle; he knows it because this core value has been passed down to him through his forebears. He is not worried about the heavy price he is paying now, nor is he concerned that the seed will not grow. He is diligent in his work, knowing full well that what he plants today will grow tomorrow. Former

> It is the fruit of the hard times that will carry the farmer through the good times.

generations have handed him the faith from which he operates. Experience has given him the confidence to labor, knowing his labor will not be in vain.

Not everyone has the foresight of the farmer when they are dealing with life's hardships. But without it, you will end up bankrupt, like the lazy man. Let's next take a look at the lifestyle of the lazy man, who does not understand the principle of sowing now to reap later.

The Lazy Man

The lazy man lacks vision. He does not have generations of wisdom to fall back on. He sleeps during the heat of the day because he believes that the only things a hard day's work in the sun produces are blisters and heatstroke. He has no expectancy of good times or abundance in the future; in fact, he is not concerned about the future because he is too busy trying to survive today while exerting the least amount of effort possible. This lazy man has not been taught the secret of hard times; he only knows of the punishment that hard labor dishes out.

To the lazy man, his view of the world justifies his lifestyle. To him, it seems better to beg through the winter than to sacrifice in the spring. A man with this mentality will never be full. He walks around in a state of spiritual and emotional anemia, dying to get what others have. Crisis follows him around like collectors chase debt. I am not talking about the hungry who are sowing from the seed they are getting; I am talking about the habitual taker who has no vision for sowing. To be honest, many of us have an area in our lives where our outlook is like the lazy man's view. It may not represent our whole life—just one area.

> To be honest, many of us have an area in our lives where our outlook is like the lazy man's view.

The "poverty mentality" has plagued the minds of our generation. This often operates like a hereditary disease that has been passed down through a family line. From generation to generation, it holds entire bloodlines depressed and unable to reach their full potential. The poverty mentality says, *There is never enough. No matter what I do, I'm always going to be like this.* It also says things like, *If only I had a hand-up like everyone else in this world, I would make something of myself.* This jaded mentality is a prison of hopelessness. Once it has fully set in, its victims will be completely unmotivated and without vision.

Taking the Long View

Let's go back and look again at the farmer's view of life, from which we can glean some practical steps to take. In the farmer's view, I can see three steps that will help us overcome the poverty mindset and grab hold of the fruit of the hard times. The first step I have found is that we can *sow with tears of joy.* The second step is that we can realize that *today is the day*. And the third step is that we must recognize *the joy of trials*. Let's map out each of these steps further.

Step 1: Sow with Tears of Joy

Psalm 126:5 says, "Those who sow in tears shall reap in joy" (NKJV). This Scripture paints a picture of what happens when a farmer plants in a hard season. During the agricultural age, if the rains failed to come and the crops ceased to grow, the year's harvest would then be meager at best. Often, there would not be enough seed from the previous year's harvest to both plant a full crop and feed the family. The farmer and his family were then stuck facing a dilemma: Should they eat the seed they need for planting and thus avoid starvation for the time being? Or should they go without food now and plant the seed in order to have a harvest for the next year?

> The reason the farmer was sowing seed with tears of joy was because as he planted the seed, he was seeing both his family's hunger and the crop that would break the poverty cycle.

You can tell from this psalm that this farmer had long-range vision. Without vision, he would have given way to the yearning in his stomach, and he and his family would have eaten their way into poverty. But the reason he was sowing seed with tears of joy was because as he planted the seed, he was seeing both his family's hunger and the crop that would break the poverty cycle.

Some people are stuck in a perpetual downward spiral in life. Their daily focus has slowly turned from making a difference in the world to avoiding starvation. It is easy to fall into this mentality. Laziness (lack of vision) can creep into all areas of life, slowly creating complacency. Without vision, you will settle for a hot meal at the end of the day instead of a planted field that will eventually yield a plentiful harvest. Success will be whittled down to a full belly and a warm bed at night. Because you have sown no seed, there will be no harvest for the future. You have eaten every bit of your seed to preserve your life now.

If you want to break this cycle, you have to understand this principle: *In the present, you will always have to sacrifice to have a brighter future.*

Step 2: Today Is the Day

One of Benjamin Franklin's famous quotations tells us never to leave something for tomorrow that we can accomplish today. Today is the day. There will never be another today, and each day is a gift from God that we will never be given again.

There is something beneficial that happens when you are diligent with the time and tasks you have been given. When you have accomplished today the things that you were supposed to get done, you have effectively set yourself up for success in more than one way. The first way is that it actually creates momentum in your life. Momentum is the driving force that makes average seem exceptional and common seem profound. I witness this effect all the time in my environment at church. Someone without momentum in his or her life will get up on stage and share revelation, and usually it will impact just a few people. In the same fashion, a person with momentum will get up and share a similar revelation, and the effect on the crowd is dramatically increased.

> There is something beneficial that happens when you are diligent with the time and tasks you have been given.

Why? Because momentum equals favor. When someone has momentum in his or her life, others recognize it and are attracted to the success, confidence and productivity they see.

The opposite effect is at work, however, for the person who does not accomplish tasks when they ought to be done. Even if you accomplish a task a day late, in your mind you know that you should have done it the day before. Instead of creating momentum so that you feel successful when the task is completed, the delay creates a thought process that says you are behind and are trying to catch up, instead of that you are ahead and are taking over. Living a lifestyle of catching up all the time creates a sense of hopelessness and low self-esteem.

A second way this principle of diligence creates success is called sowing and reaping. In the book of Matthew, Jesus shares a parable of a master who was leaving his home to go on a journey. Before he left, he entrusted his property to his servants. One servant received five talents (a form of money), the second servant two talents and the third one talent, according to their respective abilities. After a while, the master returned and asked each servant to give an account of his investment. The first two servants each explained that they put their money to work and doubled it for him. But the last servant did not do as good a job with what he had been given. In fact, he explained that he had buried the money in a hole, knowing that this master was a hard and unpleasant man.

Long story short, the master condemned the third servant, calling him wicked and lazy. Then he took that servant's one talent and gave it to the servant who had increased what he had been given the most. But the most powerful part of this whole parable is what Jesus says at the end: "For whoever has will be given more, and they will have an abundance. Whoever does not have, even what they have will be taken from them" (Matthew 25:29).

At first glance, those last few words seem rather harsh. But what Jesus is really saying is that there is a blessing for each person who is a good steward of what he or she has been given, regardless of whether it is large or small. No matter where you are today, you have an opportunity to take what you have been given and grow it. I actually believe that the greatest challenge for a lot of people is not laziness or lack of vision, but rather that they have no idea what to do next. The key to taking ground today is to stop and ask yourself what is hindering you from becoming whole. What is holding you back from God's original plan for your life?

I recently sat in on a training session in which the speaker taught about the importance of time management. Now, I am about as excited about time management as the Eskimos are about global warming. I have actually had to learn how to love my calendar. Needless to say, it has been a slow and painful process. But in that meeting the other day, we were learning about the benefit of prioritizing our lives and our calendars by importance, rather than letting worthless demands dictate our schedules.

> The key to taking ground today is to stop and ask yourself what is hindering you from becoming whole.

Most of the time, we get caught up in attending to needs that have no effect on and no benefit to our future. For example, I cannot tell you how many times I have talked to people who have major boundary issues in their life, yet they have never read a book, listened to a podcast, gone to a counselor or even spent any amount of time actually trying to fix their problem. Those same people spend countless hours watching episodes of their favorite shows on Netflix or reading magazines as if God Himself wrote them. In general, we spend very little time actually focusing on and working on the things that will bring us the most return. The average person therefore has no idea how to change and grow, because he or she spends very little time focusing on it.

As a young father, I can remember how powerless I felt against the demands of my small children. My son in particular had a way of pushing buttons I did not even know I had. On several occasions, I remember walking away from one of our little talks frustrated at the fact that my son had found flaws in me that no other human being on this entire planet had ever found. It did not take me too long to realize that my son is a genius and I was in way over my head. For me, the weeks following this realization consisted of sitting down every night after the kids went to bed and listening to a course called "Love and Logic" while taking notes. I actually spent several hours each evening working on parenting principles, and then I would apply them the very next day.

Most parents have felt frustrated on some level with the challenges of parenting. But what I found throughout all the years of counseling I have done is that most people, even when they identify a problem, don't do anything about it. The Matthew 25 parable we looked at about the lazy servant addresses this very issue. Since God has entrusted me with three beautiful kids, His expectation of me is that I am going to be a good steward of what He has given me. When I diligently take care of my kids, my inheritance grows. To be completely honest, when I first

> God's expectation of me is that I am going to be a good steward of what He has given me. When I diligently take care of my kids, my inheritance grows.

started learning how to parent my kids, I was not very good at it. But because I never gave up and I practiced being a good steward of what He had given me, the Lord blessed my diligence and has since entrusted me with influencing the lives of thousands of people through my counseling and ministry.

The farmer's mentality says that there is only one today and what you do with it will be the result that you harvest tomorrow. If you are unhappy with where you are at today, it is because of what you did with your yesterday. Look at each day as a gift, regardless of how tough or how easy the day is. If you sow in tears today, you will reap in joy tomorrow. So realize that today is the day. Wake up from your slumber, wipe the sleep from your eyes and sow diligently today for a better tomorrow!

Step 3: The Joy of Trials

James 1:2–4 says, "Consider it pure joy, my brothers and sisters, whenever you face trials of many kinds, because you know that the testing of your faith produces perseverance. Let perseverance finish its work so that you may be mature and complete, not lacking anything." Here lies one of the greatest secrets to joy in the entire Bible. Yet on first glance, this seems like the most ridiculous passage. I am not sure how you operate, but the last time I was in a major trial, my first reaction was not to feel hilariously excited about it. I did not tell myself, *I think this trial is going to test my faith so that I'm not going to ever lack a thing*. Instead, my first reaction was to figure out how in the world I got into the trial, so that I could get out of it as quickly as possible.

God's process for creating wholeness in us happens through trials that strengthen our faith in Him. The only way we could possibly go through a trial and be super happy about it is if we truly believe that God causes everything to work together—including the hard situations—for good in our lives (see Romans 8:28). I know this does not sound like very much fun, but it happens to be true.

Great opportunity comes with every hard season, for those who have eyes to see it. So put the farmer's mentality into action and begin the work. There is an excitement that comes for the farmer in every season. He is not thrilled about his blisters, but he is excited about what the pain produces.

> Great opportunity comes with every hard season, for those who have eyes to see it.

I have heard it said many times that adversity pushes a great man to the top. The resistance of the hard ground produces strength in the farmer. This strength will carry him all through his life; it will be the strength he will use in his later years. The wisdom that he gains through his labor he will pass down through his family line. His faith will become their faith in their tough seasons; his sons will use his testimony to produce a harvest in their lives, and there will always be enough.

Lessons from the Life of David

I love the life of David. David was a master at being in hard seasons of life and refusing to leave his circumstances until God promoted him. He continuously used adversity as a battering ram to force his way into his destiny.

David's first victories over the lion and the bear strategically set him up for his victory over Goliath, which in turn landed him in the palace, ministering to King Saul. It was not long, however, before David's ministry to Saul ended abruptly. In fits of rage, King Saul drove David away from his kingdom and forced him to live like a vagabond, hiding in the hills and caves while Saul tried to kill him. This time in David's life would prove to be one of the most strategic advancements toward his destiny, as hundreds of outcasts rallied to him in his vulnerability.

Throughout this time, David refused to kill King Saul and take over his kingdom, even though the opportunity presented itself on more than one occasion. David understood that prematurely exiting the season God had him in would be like giving birth to a baby at twelve weeks because you are tired of the pregnancy process. It is going through a difficult process, however, that brings about maturity in our lives. Ultimately, David became one of the greatest kings in history. And the outcasts who were hiding with him became his mighty men, his protection throughout the rest of his years (you can read more of his story in 1 Samuel 17–31).

The Lord uses adversity in our lives for His purposes. He does not always deliver us from resistance, because His first concern is not our comfort. God wants us to become like Him—perfect, not lacking anything. Like the farmer, if we skip the process of breaking the hard ground and tilling the soil, the seed we scatter will not take root, but will wither and die under the scorching sun.

> It is going through a difficult process that brings about maturity in our lives.

I am assuming that if you are reading this book today, adversity is standing at your doorstep and peering in your window. I have good news for you: God is creating a way for you to be complete, not lacking anything. Your job in this season is to grab hold of hope and not let go! Like the farmer who labors to produce a crop, your joy lies in the hope of the harvest to come.

Don't Lose Hope

The writer of Hebrews said, "Now faith is the substance of things hoped for, the evidence of things not seen" (Hebrews 11:1 NKJV). If you only operate out of what can be seen, you will never be able to lay up an inheritance for your future. Without hope, without the ability to believe and trust God, it is impossible to have faith. And without faith, it is impossible to access heaven. What you believe in your heart and what you hope for will eventually be made manifest in the natural realm. If you are stuck in a poverty mindset, and if life has run you through its merry-go-round of disappointment, it is time to change what you expect. Solomon wrote, "For as he [a man] thinks in his heart, so is he" (Proverbs 23:7 NKJV).

> If you are stuck in a poverty mindset, and if life has run you through its merry-go-round of disappointment, it is time to change what you expect.

The outcome of your hard times will be what thrusts you into your destiny. The harvest you produce in adversity will provide you with fruit that will sustain you in your later years. In fact, what has been sown through the sacrifice of your youth will be passed down and carried throughout the generations.

The next time you enter a difficult season in life, take the long view, take some steps like the ones we talked about to overcome the poverty mindset and grab hold of the fruit of the hard times you are facing. Sow with tears of joy, realize that today is the day and acknowledge that there is joy in the trials. Let the plow of perseverance prepare your field of prosperity.

1. Let's step into the farmer's perspective. Read James 1 over your life and meditate on this truth: The trial that you are going through today is creating perseverance in your life, and perseverance is going to bring you to a place where you lack nothing with God.

2. It is time to gain momentum. Have you set priorities in your life? What do you need to do today, practically, that is going to bring you breakthrough for tomorrow?

3. Refer back to this chapter's "Step 2: Today Is the Day" section. In what ways are you focusing your time, effort, money and energy on the things that will bring you the biggest return today and for your future?

4. As James 1 and Philippians 4 say, the process of perseverance should always start with joy and thankfulness. This literally will help sustain you and give you energy. What are you doing to express your joy and thankfulness while in the process God has you going through right now?

FIVE

Unlocking the Inner Man

Stories are such a powerful way to distill truth for living. In the previous chapter, I told you a story about a farmer and a lazy man (a man without vision), to illustrate how our approach to the hard times in life will affect our future. I also described the parable of the talents, which illustrates the importance of being good stewards of what we have been given.

I want to begin this chapter with a powerful story, too—a modern parable about a heart that is disconnected from its circumstances. This allegory describes many men and women who have spent their whole lives never connecting to their emotions.

The Frozen Heart

Take a walk with me down a long, slender corridor, a place where life has been forgotten. The hardened walls of ice carry no ability in themselves to feel or breathe, for they have been sealed shut from the light of day. As you pass through the corridor, you can see the work of many hands. Carved deep within the walls of ice are the scars of ancient history. Murals from top to bottom tell the stories of incessant abuse and perversion that have plagued this place.

As you continue down the frozen corridor, you come to a set of steel bars and peer into a cage, unable to go any farther. Lying on the floor at your feet are thousands of words of affirmation and love, all of them worthless— shattered to pieces—while words of hate and rage claw at the cage's door, trying to find their way in. Peering through the steel bars, you see a heart torn and cold from the empty promises of falsely affectionate deceit. Upon seeing the bleeding heart, you begin to beg and plead to be let in. At the top of your lungs you cry out for mercy, but your words only echo off the ice-laden walls. There is no one here to care, no one here to hear your plea. Quickly, your pleading turns to torment as you frantically search for the keys that will unlock the cage door, for it won't be long until this cold heart you see trapped inside is frozen in time, unable ever to feel again.

As you dig through the shattered words strewn on the floor, your fingers begin to bleed. But it matters not, for somewhere in the wreckage there must be a key . . . a way in. You dig and dig until the ice-cold concrete floor meets your bleeding fingers, but still there is no way to open the cage and reach that devastated heart. In your frustration you scream at the heart, *"Who put you here? Who would leave you here to rot in this frozen grave?"*

Your words carry through the bars, sinking compassion deep into the freezing heart. At your words the heart moans aloud, for it hears only the torment of past love. Slowly, the prison bars grow thicker, and the temperature drops in the corridor. Quickly, you realize that the heart itself is the one that built this prison. No longer can it allow itself to unlock the steel cage that it took so long to fortify. No longer can it risk the torment of hope deferred and love abused.

Time is running out. The corridor is unbearably cold, and soon you will be like the heart, numb and unable to move. You have to make a decision to stay and risk the possibility of death yourself, or leave behind what was once vibrant and full of love, to die. Death is the black face of evil stealing what was never his to take.

You take a deep breath and think about your family— the wife of your youth, and your kids who so affectionately cling to you as their father. You try to breathe deeply over and over, but your breathing quickly turns to gasping as you begin to realize that you can feel nothing for your wife and kids. In terror, you examine your chest and find that your heart is gone. In a panic, you run back up the corridor to the frozen murals of ice, to the place where memories are stored. Looking high and low, you begin to examine each picture in its intricacies. There you are as a young child clinging to your father, grasping at his affirmation, yet you were never good enough. You were the son he did not need. In his lack of love for you, he broke your spirit with his words. His lack of affection was a trapper's snare, punishing your heart for wanting just a taste of consolation.

Looking over the icy panorama, you begin to realize that your whole life has been a horror of memories that leave you cold . . . a testimony of what happens to a heart that is left open to feel. Somewhere along the line, your life became a routine of slowly shutting down. After all, one does not have to feel in order to live, especially when feeling is worse than dying. You feel like crying, but there are no tears; you are too cold trapped inside yourself— inside the fortress you yourself made.

Running back to the heart, you pound on its cage, screaming again to be let in. *"Can't you see we're going to die down here?"* you shout.

The heart groans at your words but is unwilling to move. Falling to your knees, you begin to plead with it, reciting memories from your childhood: "I was there when love was abused, when all you wanted was the touch of a father. I was there when perversion became the comfort for a broken spirit . . . the only way out. I saw the pain in shutting down, knowing that it meant losing the possibility of ever bonding again. And I see the hatred you have toward me for not being able to protect you . . . for not being able to see through the deceptive lies."

For the first time in ages, the heart begins to cry at the realization that there is someone who cares—someone who sees where it has been. For even though the heart lives inside you, it is very much its own entity, needing to be explored and understood. The tears pour out, and the ice slowly melts as the heart begins to feel again. Never before has the heart felt protected enough to unlock the steel cage, but one by one the bolts begin to break as you make your heart some promises: "I promise to love you more than anyone else. I promise to find a way to protect you. I promise not to be afraid to feel, even when it hurts. And I promise never to disconnect from you again, leaving you alone to fend for yourself!"

> Even though the heart lives inside you, it is very much its own entity, needing to be explored and understood.

Leaving the corridor that day, you know a significant change has taken place inside you. You have decided to be powerful and not to hide from life anymore. You have decided both to open your heart and to guard it.

Defensive Walls of Protection

Many of us have spent our entire life not realizing what our heart really needs, and not being aware of the punishment that life has dished out. Without the ability to connect to our heart, we have no way of meeting our deepest needs. This type of living leaves us desperate for a way to cope with the onslaught of normal life, because a need unmet leads to pain. We should go on the journey of learning what our deepest needs are and how to meet them, but many of us lock our heart away instead.

No one ever begins life with the intent of locking himself or herself inside a prison of ice. After all, who wants to be unknown and alone? The process of emotionally shutting down is a person's last-ditch effort at surviving what his or her mind deems blunt-force trauma. When the trauma fails to subside, the mind has to make a decision either to go completely insane or to disconnect from the emotional side of reality.

A few years ago, I was introduced to a guy named Blake, who at that time was the only person I had ever met who was among the "living dead." Before I found out anything about him, he asked if I would sit down and help him work through some stuff. As Blake began to share that day, my eyes were opened to a world I had never seen before. Blake's early childhood memories were riddled with abuse, most of it intentionally inflicted by the ones who were supposed to love him the most. Blake explained to me that at a very young age, even before he entered school, he had decided not to feel anymore. He believed that the only people who were not hurting were people who were in heaven or people who did not feel anything.

Blake "lived" his whole childhood, right through his teen years, emotionally shut off and numb from what his heart was feeling. In fact, he said that if you had seen him on the street and tried to beat him up, he would not even have protected himself. He explained to me that people who protect themselves have something of value, and if you have something valuable, then you have something to lose. If you have something to lose, then you can feel pain.

Blake had fortified his entire heart and emotions inside a steel cage covered in ice. No words or feelings could get in, and he could feel nothing as long as the bars were in place. He was among the living dead, walking around literally not allowing himself to feel anything or care about anything in life.

I spent several weeks with Blake, chipping away at the ice-laden walls and removing the bars his heart had spent a lifetime building. Much as in the allegory I started this chapter with, Blake slowly was able to create a place where his heart was able to feel again. What I learned was that no one is too far gone, and that Blake is not an isolated case. A large number of people in our society have in some way decided to shut down their emotions. In fact, I have found that most people who have shut down did not necessarily live in a crazy home or endure a ton of abuse. But because they did not know how to deal with pain, they had to lock up some part of their heart to stay alive.

An Overprotected Heart

I once counseled a young woman who expressed an inability to fall in love. To give you some perspective, she was drop-dead gorgeous and single. Yet no matter how many men she met or how much her friends tried to help her, she maintained an idealistic view of how a romantic relationship had to happen, and she was unwilling to budge from that view. She pretty much indicated that the only way a relationship would work for her was for it to be designed by Walt Disney himself.

Over the course of the year that I worked with her, she began to have a revelation. Through my input and the consultation of many friends, she finally realized that her view of finding a man was actually sabotaging her relationships. She had purposely created an impossible list of things she needed from a husband, so that she could protect herself from ever having to risk falling in love *again*. Obviously, her past relationships had taught her lessons about love that she never wanted to repeat. But because she had no idea how to protect her heart and work through the pain, her heart did the only thing that it knew to do: It created a way to keep love out.

> The most common reason people shut down is because of their childhood upbringing. . . . They learn lessons about love and vulnerability that teach them to hide at all costs.

I have found that the most common reason people shut down is because of their childhood upbringing. As a young child, you are the most vulnerable that you will ever be to the environment around you, and you are the most powerless to change it. Because of this, kids often become victims of their parents' dysfunction. They learn lessons about love and vulnerability that teach them to hide at all costs.

The allegory we started with is a great example of what happens when people look back on their childhood and realize they were never really loved and cared for. They then begin to understand why their heart had to lock itself up in a steel cage. Because this locking away usually happens at a young age, it is common for people not even to realize as adults what actually happened . . . how their heart actually shut itself down to survive in a frozen environment.

Dysfunction develops in a world where needs go unmet and pain becomes a customary part of your daily diet. When love is given and received on a conditional basis— I will love you only if you say or do the right things— behaviors such as codependency and control become the norm. These behavioral issues manifest themselves in all kinds of ways, from rage to manipulation, even to passivity.

Although these "frozen" people live as if they have no needs, they often become masters at fulfilling everyone else's needs. On the outside, they look like Jesus as they run around and make sure everyone else is taken care of. But in reality, they have learned that having needs themselves and requiring something in a relationship are things that only lead to pain, because that is what they were taught as children. Not expressing any needs is therefore an effective, but incredibly dysfunctional, way to protect themselves from pain.

The Beauty of Emotion

There are literally hundreds of ways that people protect themselves from having to feel, and there are just as many ways that they compensate for the pain in their lives. But the important thing to realize is that God is the one who designed us with feelings. When God created humankind, He created us as a masterpiece of emotions. In the purest form, our emotions are motivators. Without them, we would not really accomplish much. Our body picks up on emotions, which are used to move us to action. When stimulated, our muscles have the ability to tense or relax, and blood vessels dilate or contract depending on the feelings coursing through our body. Our emotions therefore play a big part in motivating us to action, or deterring us from it.

On another level our minds pick up on emotions, too, which assists us in making decisions. For example, when we think about doing something that contradicts our values, our emotions will let us know that it is probably not a good idea. Even just imagining such a scenario can stimulate our emotions to let us know whether or not something feels like a good plan. Make no mistake, there are times when emotions will absolutely betray us, and not everything that feels like a good plan at the time is one. That is why it is important to know what you are feeling and to have a good partnership with the Holy Spirit so that you are walking in truth and wholeness.

> When God created humankind, He created us as a masterpiece of emotions. In the purest form, our emotions are motivators.

Without the ability to feel emotions, you would be unable to connect to the world around you. Your emotions create strong bonds of connectivity and harmony between you and your social environment. I cannot count how many times I have talked with young kids who are completely heartbroken that their parents have never spoken the words "I love you" to them. Even as an adult, the pain of living your whole life without having your parents ever emotionally connect with you is incredibly damaging. In contrast, if you look back at some of the best times in your life with your friends or family, they were probably times when you felt emotionally connected to the people who are important to you. On the most fundamental level, we are created to connect to the world around us on a heart-to-heart level.

> On the most fundamental level, we are created to connect to the world around us on a heart-to-heart level.

It is important to remember that God created both positive and negative emotions, and each of them plays a vital part in our lives. Negative emotions help keep us alive. They signal warnings and prompt us to act—from running away to avoiding others, even to fighting back. Positive emotions are so important because they actually do things like boost our immune system, promote good self-esteem and ward off depression. There are entire books written on this subject alone. Yet the basic thing to understand is that it was God's original intent that we would live connected to our own heart.

Hello, Self

When was the last time you stopped and asked yourself, *How is my heart doing today? What do I need in order to feel okay? Why do I feel the way I do? What can I do about it?* Your head and your heart are your two best advocates for creating a healthy life. Without knowledge of what is going on inside you and what your soul needs, you really have no way of fully taking care of yourself.

Most of us were never taught how to listen to our head and our heart. In fact, many of us were taught lies like "pain is weakness leaving the body," or "what doesn't kill you only makes you stronger." The truth is that whether it is physical or emotional, pain is a need begging to be met. The longer a person lives in pain, the more likely it is that his or her heart will shut down. Many of us don't even know who we are, because we have not stopped long enough to say hello to ourselves or ask ourselves, *How can I help you?* If we don't know who we are or how we are doing, how can we really share ourselves with others?

> Your head and your heart are your two best advocates for creating a healthy life.

It is tempting to avoid asking ourselves questions such as how we are doing, because sometimes this type of question can lead to feeling powerless if we don't know what to do about the answer. In the next chapter, we will learn the truth about pain and how to process through it in a healthy way. No longer do we have to live numb to the world around us or disconnect from our hearts. We can learn how to unlock our inner selves and break the damaging vows that have kept us trapped inside ourselves.

REFLECT

1. Are you fully alive, or are there parts of you that have shut down? Write down any parts of you that you feel are shut down.

2. Ask the Holy Spirit to show you when and where the trauma happened that caused you to shut off certain parts of yourself. (Reading chapter 6, just ahead, will also help you with this, so keep this question in mind as you read on.)

3. What are a few key things you believe are true about love, connection, having emotions and expressing needs?

4. Do you regularly check how your heart is doing? To help you with that, reread this chapter's final section, "Hello, Self," and spend some time each morning and evening asking yourself these questions: *How is my heart doing? What do I need in order to feel okay? Why do I feel the way I do? What can I do about it?* Asking these questions on a daily basis is key to reflecting back on your heart and emotions. (As we learn how to process pain in the next chapter, it will give you a really practical way of healing any wounds that come up in your answers and validating your own needs.)

SIX

In the Comfort
of Your Own Pain

Sit for a while with me, kick off your shoes, close your eyes and relax. Welcome to the cold weather of reality, a place that is uncomfortably painful for most of us. I promise not to leave you here in your pain too long, because I know what it is like. I have been here, too. In the last chapter, we talked about your inner self and all the different ways that your heart has tried to protect you from the onslaught of a painful reality. In this chapter, you are going to find out that reality is the only safe place to be.

In the stories in the previous chapter there was a common denominator, a common theme. The people I described did not have a great process in place for dealing with pain. If you think about it, when was the last time someone taught you how to process through pain? If you are like most people, the answer is probably never.

So, my next question for you is, "What did you do with your pain?" Stop reading for a second and actually ask yourself that question. The answer is probably a huge key to unlocking why you are the way you are.

Buried Alive

I remember one particular counseling appointment when I was working with a guy who had just returned from Iraq. Joe was a nurse in the Army, so on a regular basis he was exposed to horrific scenes of mortality. He was in my office because he could not feel anymore; he was numb to the world around him.

As Joe sat across from me, I had him close his eyes. Then I asked him, "Where did you put your emotions?"

He sat there for a while before he opened his eyes and described a devastating scene. Here is Joe's account in his own words:

I gotta dig faster! I say to myself, as if there were anyone in the field to hear me. The dirt is very cold and hard to dig a hole in, but I have begun to make some progress. The hole is about two feet deep now; I can just make out the bottom in the dim moonlight. I can hear the men somewhere in the distance, shouting and crashing through the brush; they are getting closer, but still there's time.

I am covered head to toe in blood and in the freezing mud. I shout to the moon, almost in a wail, *"I need to bury this thing before they catch me!"* The dirt and rocks have worn down my fingernails until they bleed and burn like fire. I can hear horses drawing close; the hounds are leading them straight to me! Just a few more seconds and I can shove this flesh into the hole, and no one will ever know what I did with it.

I squat just above the hole and look around like some wild animal being hunted. I can hear the hunters now. Their shouts are very close, and I can see their lights illuminating the ground around me. With my task almost complete, I pay them nothing more than a fleeting glance. I think to myself for a moment about my bare feet, the footprints I am leaving. They are an open invitation for anyone to dig up what I have so hastily buried, but I can't do anything about it now. I don't have the time.

I cram it into the hole; I shove the loose dirt and rocks back into the cavern that I have made just as a flashlight finds me. A man screams to his friends, *"There he is—we have him now!"*

I dart off into the night, running swiftly, like a bird cutting through the air. It's buried. I hope they will forget what I have put there. I pray they follow me far away. I leap into a run. I drag my bloodstained body over fallen tree trunks, and I dash through creeks; the searing cold water burns for a few short seconds. I can't worry about that now. My bare feet slap the ground hard, shaking me to my core. My feet are ripped to pieces and scream with agony at my every step, but I won't stop running. I quickly make my way down a trail into the valley below; the farmlands look so far away in the moonlight. My very desperate and abrupt exit has left the posse in utter confusion. It will take them a few minutes to regroup. I find peace in this thought.

I break through a thicket of oak trees at the bottom of the trail. On the valley floor, I reach the farmlands. I begin to push my way through the cornfields; they will provide excellent cover and keep the men from finding me quickly. The earth here is soft; it is hard to make a quick escape, and now I know that I am losing ground. I break through the far side of the cornfields, where I find an abandoned house. It will provide me a place to rest while they search within the fields. I burst through the front door, closing it behind me. I run to the window that faces the cornfield I have just come from and open it a crack so I can hear the men when they come for me. Slumping down, I lay my head up against the windowsill for a moment. I don't know how long I am there because I drift off to sleep.

I awake to a strange orange glow and a crackling sound. Dazed from sleep, I am having trouble comprehending what is happening. It strikes my mind like a lightning bolt that they set the field on fire to flush me out. The smoke is pouring into the house! Choking, I run through the living room and pass into the dining room. I smash through the back door and head for the barn. I can't hear much over the roar of the fire. I make it to the barn in a few short seconds. I round the corner; I am trying to make it past the barn and onto another field just beyond. I never see the man or the axe handle, but it finds my head in a perfect swing.

I awake to find a dozen men around me, still staring in horror at the sight before them. You see, the thing I buried, the flesh I put into the ground, it wasn't another man's. It was mine! I cut out my own heart; I couldn't bear the burden of the pain that it brought me anymore. Love that I had lost, things that I have done and seen. I had to be rid of it. Rid of it I am. The posse hunted me because they thought I had killed someone. The only thing I had killed was my ability to feel—forever. I stand up before them, blood-soaked and freezing.

A fat, bald man approaches me. He says feebly, "Son, what have you done to yourself? How are you still alive?"

I snicker at his remark. I reply in a tone that could skin a man alive, "There's nothing left for me in that piece of tired flesh. It's all that remains of a life that I want nothing more than to forget."

He steps back, unsure how to respond to me.

I lash out again, "How am I still alive, you ask? It's because of my strong will to live a life free of pain."

They bring in the reporters now; they take pictures with their fancy cameras. They write things down in their white notepads with blue lines. I can already see the picture of me in the morning paper: these men standing around me, looking triumphant. I am soaked in blood, caked and dripping with mud. A large hole is cut just below my left nipple, just the perfect size to squeeze my heart out of. Steam can still be seen pouring out of the hole, signs of a still-warm body. I am barely covered in tattered clothes, no shoes. My face is filthy, and shackles dangle from my wrists and ankles. What a sight I must be for them. They fear me in this state. I am some rabid animal that must be destroyed. I have no feelings now. The thought of a man like this scares them. It won't be easy for them to kill me. I won't make it easy for them.

Joe had buried his emotions in some hole far away, never to be seen again. The daily brutality of war was more than he could possibly handle on his own. And after he got home, without the ability and the consciousness to process through what his heart was feeling, the only other logical option was to take his heart and bury it once again.

Regardless of whether your experiences are like Joe's or like my walk through a destructive divorce, you have to have a plan for your pain. One of the greatest misconceptions people have about pain is that time heals it. They think that somehow, if they just forget about it or ignore what they are feeling or what has happened to them, it will all go away. This could not be further from the truth! If time healed, people in prison would be the most whole people in the world.

> You have to have a plan for your pain. One of the greatest misconceptions people have about pain is that time heals it.

Time is a revealer and an enabler. If you plant a seed in the ground and water it, in time it will grow and reveal its species. If you plant that same seed and never give it water, it will never grow. In the same way, if you go through the process of healing, in time you will be made whole. But if you skip the healing process, you will be left wondering why you are the way you are.

Blessed Are Those Who Mourn

Matthew wrote, "Blessed are those who mourn, for they will be comforted" (Matthew 5:4). If what this verse is saying is true, then it could also read, "Cursed are those who don't mourn, for they are not comforted." The actual process of working through pain and becoming a whole person involves acknowledging and mourning your pain.

The challenge of this type of thinking is that none of us like to sit around and think about our emotional pain. Most of the time, pain causes us to feel so incredibly powerless and hopeless that just focusing on it makes it worse. The typical response to pain, therefore, is to ignore it. Without the process of mourning, however, there is no comfort.

> The actual process of working through pain and becoming a whole person involves acknowledging and mourning your pain.

To mourn pain does not mean that you just sit there and think about it until you get really angry and overwhelmed (although this may happen as part of the process). The healthy way to mourn your pain requires a beginning and an end to the process.

It is just like a funeral, where you know that you are going to walk in and experience the life of the person who died through pictures and kind words. You also know that you are probably going to cry at the reality that he or she is gone. But finally, if you have ever experienced a death in the family, you know that the pain eventually recedes, after the tears are shed and the memories are processed.

Disarming the Inner Time Bomb

The day my wife left me, all the memories and shared experiences that used to bring me warm feelings were instantly transformed into objects of heartache. No longer were the thoughts of my wedding day or our first date happy memories. No longer did it bring me joy to think about our honeymoon night and the way I had given her my heart. I was alone, trapped inside a mind full of memories, each one of them cutting me to the core. As much as I wanted to just wake up and have it all be gone, I was stuck with all those memories inside me.

I quickly realized that memories are like time bombs. If I failed to acknowledge their presence and disarm them, they would explode inside me, creating incredible amounts of uncontrollable anger. If I let the anger out in an unhealthy way, it would hurt the ones I loved the most, my kids.

With that realization, I began to change the way I saw my pain. Memories that used to send me crashing were now welcomed in, and I carefully pondered and mourned each one until the sting was gone. This is the practice of stewardship. That's right—you have to steward every painful thought, looking at each one as a gift brought forward to make you whole. Once I overcame the fear of being in pain and I started to face each memory, I felt an excitement because every processed memory was a step toward freedom.

I can remember the first time after my divorce that I thought about my wedding day. I was in the middle of worship during a session at Bethel's school of ministry, just lying up on stage enjoying God's presence. Almost without warning, I was completely caught up in the memory of my wedding. There she was, riding in on a chocolate-brown horse led by her brother. My heart pounded in my chest as she slowly walked toward me to the soundtrack of the film *Braveheart*.

> Once I overcame the fear of being in pain and I started to face each memory, I felt an excitement because every processed memory was a step toward freedom.

Soon she was at the altar, and I was there to take her hand. The pastor spoke and we took Communion, and then in a moment we began exchanging vows. There I was, giving her my heart that I so desperately needed back. At her words my tears began to run, and the memory continued to play.

In real time, the school of ministry's worship was pounding in my ears, and the thought of her never coming back was dripping down my face. It was not long before I couldn't control myself, and my tears turned to wailing. I quickly realized that worship was going to end and I was going to be left onstage in a puddle of tears. Leaving worship, I headed upstairs to my office, thinking to myself, *I don't want to lose this memory; I want to work all the way through it.* When I finally reached my office, I quickly turned on some music that matched my mood and settled back into the memory.

I sat there that day in my office, allowing the memories of my wedding day to play in my head as I cried through the reality that it was really over. I can remember picturing her walking down the aisle over and over again, while I asked God what He wanted me to do with these thoughts. Eventually, the details of our wedding and the reality that it was over did not hold the same sting as the first time it hit. God began to answer the questions the memories brought to me, questions like *What's going to happen to my kids? Am I ever going to love again?* One by one the memories would come, each one with a different sting. And one by one I would cry through them, until the sting was gone and God had answered my questions.

Pain Doesn't Have to Stay

Throughout the process of working through my pain, I realized that without the ability to connect and feel and let out what was going on in my heart, I would have no way of being free. Most Christians have been so programmed to look only at the positive that it can easily seem like a violation to focus on and mourn their losses.

Recently, I met with a woman for a counseling appointment who said that she never cries and has a hard time expressing her needs to others. The perplexing thing about her is that she is Superwoman in the room, attending to everybody else's needs, making them feel loved and accepted. But when it comes to herself, she would rather listen to someone else than express what she is dealing with at that moment.

Sitting in my office that day, Megan began to tell me her story. Her father had died when she was really young, leaving her with an incredible amount of pain at a young age. Around the age of eighteen, she received a phone call that her mother had died in a car accident. Megan was left scared and alone. In one day, she had gone from making plans to hang out with her mom to being left alone in this world.

> Most Christians have been so programmed to look only at the positive that it can easily seem like a violation to focus on and mourn their losses.

Shortly after her mother died, Megan's friends and family gathered together to attend the funeral. Kind words were spoken and beautiful songs were sung, and soon it was all over and done with. After the funeral, Megan's friends gathered around her and took her into the living room of her house for a time of worship and praise. They felt as though she needed to start a new chapter in her life and worship her way out of this terrible time.

The more I listened to Megan, the more I realized that she had never allowed herself to mourn the loss of her parents. And because Megan had never mourned, she was never free of the pain. Megan's friends had great intentions in wanting her to be free of pain, to feel joy and to be able to praise. But what they did not realize is that by not allowing her to mourn her loss and work through the pain, she was stuck with it.

Megan had never allowed herself to access all of her heart, because she believed that the pain would never go away. It was pointless, she thought, even to go there. She was trapped inside the façade of never feeling sad, but only acting happy. In reality, her heart was screaming for someone to acknowledge the pain.

> Only allowing ourselves to be happy is as dysfunctional as only allowing ourselves to feel pain. God created every emotion, and each one has a specific purpose.

Only allowing ourselves to be happy is as dysfunctional as only allowing ourselves to feel pain. As we learned in the previous chapter, God created every emotion, and each one has a specific purpose.

Megan and I spent a large portion of our time in that counseling appointment facing the reality that her mom and dad were never going to come back. I had her do some homework like write letters to her mom about how she felt the day she died, and journal about how it felt to get that phone call. Megan began to learn that she was not alone in her pain; God had answers for where she was at and what she needed. Over time, through processing the reality of loss and connecting to her heart, she was able to unlock her tears and face the reality that she so dreaded. To this day, Megan remains free from the pain of not knowing herself and from the feeling of being alone in this world.

Purging the Pain

With reality often comes the onslaught of emotions that have been all bottled up inside. As I said before, the average Christian will want to dumb down what he or she is actually feeling because somehow it seems like a sin to have any other thoughts besides happy ones.

When I started processing through my own failed marriage, I began to experience a myriad of emotions from anger and hatred to sorrow and grief. Often, they would manifest in different ways. What I allowed myself to do was be brutally honest with what I really felt about what had happened to me.

If you remember back to chapter 3, "Justice Served," you know that my heart was for my ex-wife's well-being and wholeness. But for myself, I could not shove away or hide the fact that I felt terribly wronged and ripped off. I spent several months writing sad songs and strikingly honest letters about what had happened and how I felt— letters that I never sent to her. For weeks, I would wake up every night around three in the morning with poetry going through my head. I gave myself permission to yell, scream or write letters about what she had done and how wrong it was, as long as what I was doing in the process was not going to hurt anyone else. (Of course, I had to make sure the kids did not hear me.)

By being honest with myself about what was going on inside me, in the privacy of my own home I was able to purge the emotions I was feeling without hurting anyone else around me. I have found that over and over again, people who go through tremendous amounts of pain and never let themselves process through it in the safety of their own home usually end up exploding at the wrong time.

> By being honest with myself about what was going on inside me, in the privacy of my own home I was able to purge the emotions I was feeling without hurting anyone else around me.

The emotions I expressed through a song or a poem were not a commentary on how I wanted to feel about my ex-wife or where I was planning on staying forever. Rather, they were snapshots of how I was feeling in that moment. Because I spent a lot of time being honest with myself in the moment and processing it out loud, when I would encounter her in person, I did not feel an angry bomb inside wanting to explode.

A Child Will Lead Them

We live in a world where our superheroes are made of cobalt steel. They are impervious to the natural laws of humanity, able to take on the hordes of hell with only a flaming arrow and then leave completely unscathed.

These heroes are broadcast before our eyes and imprinted on our minds as being at the top of society's hierarchy. Our women adore them. Our men, wanting to somehow be like them, are taught to praise their cold-heartedness as a badge of honor. These "heroic" super-men we see on the screen feel no pain, fear no evil and are able to drop a woman like their last bad habit.

As well, many parents have done a fine job of reinforcing in their children the belief system modeled by these superheroes that it is not normal to be vulnerable, and it is especially not okay to show emotion. In many homes, the children's ability to be honest about their feelings is incredibly limited because that is not what their parents are modeling. And in most homes, emotions are hidden like unconfessed sins. This unrealistic view of humanity has contributed heavily to the desensitization of our emotions.

Yet long before you were taught that heroes don't feel pain, and long before you were taught that family members hide their hearts, back in your childhood God taught you how to work through pain. If you have ever watched young children play together, you know it is only a matter of time before some exchange between them becomes the final straw that stops the fun, and then the crying begins. In my house, it often looks as though one of the older kids has somehow taken advantage of the younger one. Without even being in the same room as the kids, I can already tell what is happening by the high-pitched wailing coming from the other room. Usually, it requires my presence to resolve the issue at hand.

The interesting thing about these interactions is not what happens during the conflict, but what happens after.

My youngest, who can cry so that the whole neighborhood can hear him, is back playing happily with the other kids again in only a matter of minutes. How does this happen?

If this were a group of adults, the person who has been taken advantage of would need days or weeks to recover. Children have an inherent ability to work through heartache, however, because they have the right belief system. No one has taught them yet that it is not okay to show emotion, so without even thinking about it, as soon as they feel pain they begin to cry. Their crying purges the emotions of hurt they are feeling in the moment. And once their crying is done, the emotion is dealt with and they get on with life, happy as can be.

> Children have an inherent ability to work through heartache, because they have the right belief system. No one has taught them yet that it is not okay to show emotion.

Someone once said, "When you cry, you get all caught up," and they were right. Real men and women cry. What we have been taught through the media and from our parents about not crying and not being emotional has to change. The hero made of cobalt steel is all rusted inside. And the coldhearted Lone Ranger dad is riding his horse off into the sunset, looking for his heart. God created in us the ability to cry because He knew we would need a way of purging our pain. If we don't allow ourselves the right to get out what is on the inside, it stays bottled up in our souls and hardens our hearts. If we stay hurt long enough, eventually we will be overcome by bitter lies and vicious vows.

Exposing a Harmful Belief System

Lies take form in a world where people are punished for showing emotion or where there is no relief for the pain. Are you numb? Do you walk around wishing you could feel more, but you cannot? Do the words "I love you" said out loud send an awkward burn through your body? Or does the thought of sharing your needs with another person seem pointless or weak? These are all signs that you are operating under a harmful belief system of lies.

John, the apostle of love, wrote, "There is no fear in love, but perfect love casts out fear. For fear has to do with punishment, and whoever fears has not been perfected in love" (1 John 4:18 ESV). If you could pluck the fear out of your belief system, you would quickly find that you have been a puppet on a string, being danced through this life by the fear that is acting as your master. Your thoughts, words and actions have all been polluted by the fear of punishment or by an unfounded lie.

Let me explain. Megan, the woman at the beginning of the chapter, whose parents had died, did not allow herself to cry or express needs. When she told me this, I had her close her eyes and I asked her to tell me the first thing that popped into her head.

Megan looked up at me and said, "I believe that if I start crying, I won't stop."

Then I asked Megan what she believed to be true about pain. She quickly answered, "That there is no cure for pain."

Previous to our conversation, Megan had never consciously thought through the fact that she believed that crying never ends and that there is no cure for pain. Megan was living a life bound by fear and controlled by the master of lies. Without uprooting the lies, she would have remained imprisoned for life.

I have found that we Christians process so much that we talk ourselves out of what we really believe. But when Megan told me the first thing that popped into her mind when she closed her eyes, I knew it was what she really believed in her subconscious to be true. One thing we have to understand is that we do not just operate out of our conscious state of mind. Rather, the decisions we make and the way we behave are often manifestations of our subconscious thought processes.

I remember feeling anxiety one day so dreadfully that I could not get it to lift. It was like a bad dream that I had woken up from and could not shake. Finally, I got tired of feeling that way and retreated to my bed for a nap in the middle of the day, hoping to get some relief from the tension. While lying in bed, I began to ask the Holy Spirit why I was feeling such anxiety.

What He answered shocked me: *You use anxiety as a tool. You've partnered with it to help you.*

Now, I am not sure about you, but there is no way on God's green earth that I want to make anxiety any type of partner of mine. That would be like making my bed in an alligator nest! So I said to the Holy Spirit, *How did I make anxiety my partner?*

He said, *You wait until the last minute to get things done, until you feel anxiety. Once you feel anxiety, you're motivated to accomplish tasks that you've been neglecting.*

> I have found that we Christians process so much that we talk ourselves out of what we really believe.

Lightbulbs began to go off in my head as He revealed the partnership I had formed with anxiety. Many people have done the same thing with fear. They build partnerships with fear to protect themselves from rejection. Fear has told them things like *If you try to be yourself, you'll be rejected.* Or like *The only way to get through this time is to medicate yourself with pornography.* Or even deceptions like *No one else knows how you feel; no one really understands you.*

Lies like the ones that Megan believed about pain imprison the soul and make you a powerless puppet of fear. But perfect love casts out all fear.

The most powerful thing you can do for yourself when you are bound by fear is to allow God's perfect love to come in and be your master. His love literally drives out the lies that have kept you bound and locked up. But first you must find out how you have partnered with fear.

When Megan told me she believed that if she started crying, she would never stop, I asked the Holy Spirit to tell her the truth. The Holy Spirit began to reveal to her that if she allowed herself to grieve and feel emotion, she would become whole. We also asked the Holy Spirit if He would show her the truth about pain. He showed her that pain is not something that is incurable, but that it is actually easily taken care of.

> The most powerful thing you can do for yourself when you are bound by fear is to allow God's perfect love to come in and be your master.

When I found out that I had come into partnership with anxiety, I had to do the same thing that the Holy Spirit taught Megan. I had to break the covenant that I had made with fear. This is a simple process of renouncing the lie that you have believed to be true and taking on God's truth in place of it.

Practice Creates Courage

The important part of all this is that you must realize that while you can renounce lies and break partnerships all day long, if you don't change your actions, you have really done nothing to transform yourself. For example, when I finished the counseling appointment with Megan, I sent her home to connect with her pain and learn how to cry. In doing so, she broke the shackles of fear that had held her bound for so long.

In my case, the day I found out that anxiety had become my partner, I had a decision to make: *Do I learn to handle things on time, or am I going to procrastinate the way I've always done?* I could not break the partnership with anxiety and keep taking the same actions I had taken before. My behavior had to reflect my new belief system.

If you recognize yourself in this chapter, you will now realize that it is the lying tongue of accusation that has kept you locked up in your fear and pain. In order to truly break free, you need to begin to ask yourself some questions about your belief system and break the partnerships you have made. If you have never been able to show your emotions, ask yourself what you believe will happen if you show them. If you have always been angry, ask yourself what you believe will happen if you put down your anger. If you have never been able to say the words "I love you," ask yourself what you believe will happen if you tell the people around you that you love them.

When you ask yourself these questions, chances are good that you will start to find out the truth about why you are the way you are. Once you have done this and have found the lies, it is time to ask the Holy Spirit what the truth is about the lies you have believed. Once you have renounced the lies and have accepted the truth, it is time to change your thought processes and your daily patterns.

The most common expectation I have found in the counseling I have done is that people want results in "pill" form. They come in with major life issues and expect me to hand them two magic pills that, if taken three times

> In order to truly break free, you need to begin to ask yourself some questions about your belief system and break the partnerships you have made.

a day, will make every problem disappear. Obviously, this is not even close to how it works. The truth is that the very thing you are afraid of is the thing you are probably going to have to do. The good news is that with practice comes courage.

The key to getting completely well in a particular area is to strengthen yourself in that area. For example, if you have spent your whole life shut down because you are afraid of being rejected and hurt, then I would suggest that you read a book on how to set appropriate boundaries, and that you get some teaching on how to communicate your feelings so that you will be on your way to becoming a powerful person in this area.

If you have been afraid to cry and process emotion, then I would highly recommend keeping a journal and allowing yourself to sit with God and process through your past pain. Allow Him to answer questions about things that have carried so much hurt. I even recommend writing letters you never send and poems that only you read, to help you process your pain.

The Boundary Lines for Health

A couple of the most common questions I am asked are, "How often should I process through my pain? What are the boundaries I need to keep in place to make sure that I'm staying healthy through the process?" Eventually, people need to work through every painful or fearful thought or memory they have, because anything they are afraid to look at will ultimately keep them bound. But processing through pain is a lot like lifting weights. If you lift weights every day, all day long, without giving your body a break, instead of getting stronger you will actually break down your body to the point where you cannot function. If you process through your pain every day, all day long, and never take a break emotionally, you will be on your way to emotional breakdown. You will become so tired and weak that depression may set in.

Anytime you find yourself depressed, most likely you have believed a lie. Earlier in this chapter, I talked about warding off lies. Do you remember chapter 4, where I wrote about the fruit of the hard times? Anytime you start to feel hopeless, you need to go back and reread that chapter. Then have your friends remind you about your true destiny and what God says about you. It is also important when you are working through stressful seasons that you eat right, sleep well, exercise and have fun. I have found that most people who have breakdowns failed to take these simple steps.

Let me be clear here that when I talk about processing through every thought, I am specifically referring to events that still cause you pain, not something that is long past healed up and pain free. It is important to remember that pain was never meant to be a lifestyle—something you live with forever. Rather, pain helps you define a problem so that it can be exterminated from your life. Overemphasizing pain can create a martyr complex and become a way of life for you, instead of pain becoming a tool that points out brokenness in you so that it can be mended.

Before moving on to the next chapter, take time to really work through any pain you feel in your heart. (The "Reflect" section just ahead will help you do that.) You have to remind yourself that every painful thought can be a gift that leads you toward wholeness. Through the process of mourning your pain and replacing lies with truth, you are walking toward emotional health. In the next chapter, we will see how forgiveness partners with truth to heal our hearts and free our souls.

REFLECT

Look back to what you wrote at the end of chapters 3 and 5 at any area in which you still have unresolved pain. Then I want you to follow the six steps below to begin your journey of healing.

First step: Acknowledge the pain.
- Journal, vent, verbally process and acknowledge the pain of what is happening to your heart.
- After all the pain is acknowledged, take *one* thought, memory, feeling or emotion and sit with it.

Second step: Process this *one* thought.
- Whatever emotion and feelings come up from it, process it. Processing could look like journaling, talking to a safe friend or anything that will help you work through what is going on inside. Take no concern for your language or "being nice." This is your chance to get *all* the anger out concerning this *one* memory.
- Reassess what your heart is feeling, what you are thinking and what you are experiencing.

Third step: Once you have processed that *one* memory and there is nothing left to say about it, all your emotion on it will be exhausted and you should be able to see a theme emerge.

- Identify the one phrase or feeling that is repeated.
- Once you have that theme, take it to God in the next step.

Fourth step: Talk to God about the particular pain or "theme" you have identified.

- Ask, *What do You think, God, about the way I am hurting?* Once you ask, the Lord will give you an answer for what you are angry about or what you are feeling.
- Once you hear the heart of God, you will be able to see through His eyes and will be ready to move into the next step.

Fifth step: Ask, *God, how do You see this person who was responsible for the pain?*

- Feel the compassion that will come from seeing this person through God's eyes.
- Experiencing the compassion and the promises of God for this person and hearing what He says about the situation will then enable you to *forgive* the person for all the things you wrote down about your feelings, pain and emotion.

Sixth step: *Repeat* this process for *each* emotion, memory and thought that comes up.

- Do this until your bitterness turns into compassion in each situation.
- Remember that trust and forgiveness are not the same thing (as we will talk more about in the next chapter). You may not ever be able to trust a person who violated you, but in this process you are finding true justice by extending forgiveness to that person because Christ purchased forgiveness on the cross for you.

SEVEN

The Power of Forgiveness

Jody Bell was a beauty queen of sorts. She was young, with smooth, shiny hair, a great complexion and incredible beauty. So beautiful, in fact, that it became a detriment to her. Having an absentee father, and only a distraught mother to fall back on, she became a master at using her physical attributes to draw men in to fill her needs.

One after another the violations came, as Jody's need to feel loved dramatically increased. And with each violation of her conscience came the onslaught of lies. It did not take long for her party lifestyle to drain the beauty of her innocence away. Like a gift that had to be repackaged constantly, she no longer felt special. She began to see herself through words like *slut* and *whore*. She had painted her face red, so to speak, like the Bible's infamous Jezebel (see 2 Kings 9:30), and now her only true friends were regret and self-hatred, which accompanied her every moment of the day.

The pain of losing herself was unbearable. She hated life, and even more than that, she hated herself. In her late teens, she began to cut her arms to express the misery she felt inside. Cutting became a way of life, the only escape for a girl who now hated even her own skin. Her self-accusations all pointed to the fact that she was all used up and no longer worth anything. After all, who would love someone who had carved deep scars into her own arms?

> The hardest person to love and forgive is most often yourself.

Jody's story is not that uncommon. Although the details may be different, the truth remains the same: The hardest person to love and forgive is most often yourself.

Perhaps you see yourself in this story, or in parts of this story. Your poor decisions have brought you and the ones you love misery. And because it was you who made the decisions, you are the only one to blame. Regret is like a mortal wound that keeps you trapped in the past, slowly bleeding the life from you. Until the wound is completely healed, your future will always be tainted by regret and self-hatred.

Guilt and Shame

There are two other emotions that keep close company: guilt and shame. Some time ago, I spent a year helping a men's sexual purity group for addicts. These kinds of men come from all walks of life. Some are rich, some are poor, some have had great parents and others have lived terrible lives. But most of the men who sat in that room were actually heroes of mine. They were the ones who acknowledged that their problem was much greater than they could handle themselves.

Over the course of several months, I spent a lot of time teaching these men how to break the cycle of destruction in their lives. But there was one night in particular that stands out to me. I was explaining about the power that shame holds over us. Then I had each man close his eyes, and I asked, "How many of you are dealing with shame right now?"

This particular night there were probably several dozen men in the room, and every man except for three raised a hand. Then I told them to ask the Holy Spirit why they had kept shame in their life. After a few minutes of silence, I began to ask each man what the Holy Spirit had shown him.

The first guy who spoke had been free from the bonds of pornography for several months, if not a year. But prior to coming into this group, he had lost his whole family to his addiction. I asked him what the Holy Spirit had shown him. If he was free of pornography, why did he still have shame in his life?

He sat there for a second and thought before answering sheepishly, "The Holy Spirit showed me that I've kept shame around so that people would think I was really sorry for what I've done. If I saw any of the friends I had hurt the most and I acted happy around them, I believed they would no longer think I had repented or was sorry for what I did."

I then proceeded to ask the Holy Spirit to show this man where he had put his identity. Thinking for a second, he said, "It's in other people's pockets!"

"That's right!" I said. "If people close to you had forgiven you and were happy, you would forgive yourself and be okay with who you are. But because some of them you are the closest to have chosen to live in bitterness, you feel guilty about feeling free and happy, knowing what you've done!"

That night, each man discovered that shame was a façade, a protection he had been using to make the world see him in a certain light. One of the most powerful revelations anyone had that night was when one guy saw that he had used shame to keep him in heaven. He started out by saying, "If I were to go on a trip, the very first thing I would put in my bag would be shame. I can't remember a day that I've ever gone without it."

This particular man's earliest childhood memories were of sitting around waiting for his dad to finish looking at his porn so that he could play with him. Obviously, the sins of his father passed down to him, and like his dad, he had been bound by pornography since his adolescence.

I asked this guy, "What do you mean when you say shame is keeping you in heaven?"

He explained that the feeling of shame reminds him every day of how horrible he felt when he looked at pornography. Without the feeling of shame, he believed that he would just go right back to it.

Each of these men learned about the destructive power of shame that night. Even though many of them had been free of pornography for months and had repented and asked for forgiveness, they still carried shame around as though it were a gift to them. In reality, shame is a fiery dart shot by the devil himself, designed to keep a person bound in sin. Given an opportunity, shame will mask itself as your best friend, and it will convince you that it is only there to help you. All the while, it is stealing your freedom and raping your identity.

Sin is the devil's hand that disfigures heaven's masterpiece—the human soul—into a broken-down corpse. Satan's lies and accusations are laced with just enough truth that the pill is easy to swallow. But anytime you have a thought in your head about you that did not come from the heart

> Given an opportunity, shame will mask itself as your best friend, and it will convince you that it is only there to help you.

of God, you are trespassing against your own body. Paul said, "For all have sinned and fall short of the glory of God" (Romans 3:23). It was for this purpose that Christ died and gave Himself on the cross, so that we would no longer live bound by the laws of sin, but would live free in our God-given identity as sons and daughters of the living King.

Regardless of what you have done, the same freedom that was extended to me and set me free of unforgiveness will also set you free. When you understand the grace of Christ and what He did for you on the cross, the shackles of guilt and shame are removed because Christ has already paid for your sin.

Repentance and Root Issues

To be fully free and whole when you are the one who committed the crime, you have to extend the same forgiveness to yourself that you would extend to someone else, and you have to love yourself into wholeness again. To get to that place, you have to gain the right understanding of repentance. If you don't figure out what the real problem is (your root issues), you will constantly be stuck managing a cycle of pain. And without solving the reasons why you don't love yourself, or why you have allowed guilt and shame to rule your life, you can desire to be different all day long, but nothing will change, because the cycle of sin continues to repeat itself.

Just the other day, I counseled a guy who was struggling with pornography. He told me that he usually looks at porn about once a month or so. After listening to his story, I simply asked, "What do you feel like right before you look at porn?"

He answered, "I feel lonely and out of control."

I wanted to help him figure out where the loneliness and the feeling of being out of control were coming from, so I asked, "What was your childhood like? Tell me about your parents."

He explained, "My dad left when I was young, and even though he's in my life now, we don't have a deep connection at all. My mom didn't quite know how to handle the divorce, so in her best efforts to cope, she moved us from place to place my whole life."

As his past began to unfold before me, it became strikingly clear why he felt lonely and out of control. The most important people in his life (his mom and dad) were emotionally distant. When he needed them the most, they were not there to help him. To make matters worse, his mother's inability to settle down created in him a feeling of hopelessness, since living out of boxes and never being able to settle down and plant roots created an incredible feeling of loneliness and instability. As a young child, because of his lack of connection with people he had no way of filling his need for intimacy. As an adult, pornography became his escape from feeling powerless and unknown.

Before he came into my office, this guy thought he had a pornography problem. When he left my office, he realized that pornography was a symptom of a much greater problem. He had never learned how to get his needs met through healthy relationships. Shame told him that if he asked someone for help, he would be looked on as irresponsible and ultimately be rejected. Now he knew that he needed to repent

> Living out of boxes and never being able to settle down and plant roots can create an incredible feeling of loneliness and instability.

and change the way he thought about relationships and life. He needed to learn how to get his needs met from God and the community that surrounded him, so that he could get free from his cycle of destruction and guilt.

Finding Full Freedom in Forgiveness

Forgiveness is one of the most misunderstood and mis-used truths in the Kingdom. I have literally met hundreds of people who have spent years trying to forgive people. Although their efforts were genuine and their hearts were right, they continued to struggle with bitterness and of-fense for years.

Forgiveness does not mean that you have to feel great about what happened to you, nor does it mean that you have to reconcile with the violating party. Neither does it mean that you ever have to trust a person who violates you. Trust and forgiveness are not the same thing. For example, if a woman is raped in a dark alley, she must forgive the rapist; otherwise, hatred and bitterness will eat her from the inside out. But she never has to be alone with that man again. Trust is earned through relationship, but forgiveness was purchased by Christ on the cross.

Extending forgiveness means that you give God permission to get justice on your behalf, and you release people from your judgment and from your attempts to get justice through punishment. (Remember, we talked about true justice in chapter 3, and about how to process pain in chapter 6). I have discovered in working with many people that if they process pain correctly and then ask the Holy Spirit how He sees the violating party, He will give them compassion for that person or persons.

Most people say things like, "Forgiveness is like an onion; you peel and peel and peel until someday the hurt is gone." I don't know about you, but I hate peeling onions! The reason why trying to forgive can feel like being on a merry-go-round that reeks of onions, then, is because forgiveness without compassion is almost useless. Compassion literally activates true forgiveness, therefore releasing you from the emotional and spiritual bondage of unforgiveness.

> Trust and forgiveness are not the same thing. . . . Trust is earned through relationship, but forgiveness was purchased by Christ on the cross.

Forsaken for Our Sake

Jesus was forsaken so that we could be accepted. When He died on the cross, He did not put His fingers into His ears, so to speak, and say to God the Father, "La, la, la, I'm not thinking about You punishing Me." Imagine for a moment how badly Jesus, who had been at His Father's side throughout eternity past, must have felt at the crucifixion, when His Father abandoned Him. He cried out, "My God, my God, why have you forsaken me?" (Matthew 27:46).

For the first time ever, the eternal Son felt separated from the Father. Jesus, having taken the sin of the whole world upon Himself, experienced the anguish that sin brings because sin separates us from the Father. The grief of abandonment was worse than the pain of crucifixion.

The Bible says, "They offered Jesus wine to drink, mixed with gall; but after tasting it, he refused to drink it" (Matthew 27:34). Gall may have been a painkiller, and wine was a well-known painkiller. Christ refused the wine and gall because beyond wanting to die for our sins, I believe He also wanted our pain to die with Him—so He refused to numb His suffering. Living with pain is therefore a violation of the cross. We only embrace pain long enough to discover its root cause and apply the cure. We don't have to be afraid of pain, because it is an enemy that was defeated at Calvary.

> We only embrace pain long enough to discover its root cause and apply the cure. We don't have to be afraid of pain, because it is an enemy that was defeated at Calvary.

If you are born again and you are still dealing with something from the past that is causing you pain, refer back to chapter 6 and work through that hurt. Great freedom comes when we realize all that Christ accomplished for us. Out of that realization, we have compassion for the people who have wronged us. It is in this place that I have found the most victory in my life and in the lives of those around me.

Our Process of Forgiveness

There are many people who have not taken full advantage of Jesus' finished work on the cross. Consequently, they suffer for themselves instead of experiencing the full power of Christ's redemption. This point was driven home to me again the other night when I ministered to a young lady in line for prayer at our church.

Unbeknownst to me at first, a young man had taken cruel advantage of her when she was a kid. The second I started to pray for her, I could tell she did not love herself. I quietly whispered, "Repeat after me: *I love myself.*"

My words caused her to tremble as the pain inside her began to well up. She had been carrying around this torment for years, but it had been suppressed by the lies that bound her. Reluctantly, she repeated, "*I . . . I . . . I love myself.*"

Then I said, "Now say *I forgive myself.*"

With her chin quivering, she repeated the words after me, "*I forgive myself.*"

I then told her, "Say *I am fully loved.*"

Once again she took a deep breath, trying to control the emotions that were beginning to overwhelm her. "*I am fully loved,*" she said.

I proceeded to walk her through acknowledging her pain. She was fighting hard to keep from feeling the pain buried deep inside. I had her repeat after me, "*I renounce the lie that it's not okay to feel pain. I renounce the lie that crying is weakness. I renounce the lie that it's wrong to think about what happened to me.*"

As we got to the last statement, I could tell that the pain was completely overwhelming her. Her whole body was shaking, and she was starting to say that she could not think about it. I told her, "In your mind, I want you to tell the young man who violated you how he made you feel when he did that."

She remained quiet. I could tell that she was beginning to press through her pain, because she was getting angry and more emotional as time went by. Suddenly, she burst out yelling in the prayer line, "*I hate you! I hate you for what you did to me! I hate you for stealing my innocence and for using peer pressure to trap me!*"

I waited as she went on like this for a while. Then I said to her, "I want you to ask the Holy Spirit how He sees this young man."

She paused for a bit to listen to the Holy Spirit, and then she said, "He loves him like He loves me!"

At this point, she began to understand that even though she felt hatred and heartache toward the young man, God loved him the same as He loved her. After she connected with the pain of her past circumstances and verbalized how destructive this guy's actions had been toward her, and after she asked the Holy Spirit how He saw him, suddenly she felt compassion for him and was ready to take the next step.

I began to walk her through forgiveness by having her repeat after me, "*I forgive you for violating me. I forgive you for stealing my innocence. I forgive you for taking what was not yours to take, and for being selfish.*"

I spent a while walking her through each trespass, and then we prayed a prayer of blessing over both of them. She left the prayer line that night completely revived, having the weight of her emotions about her past lifted off her. For the first time in years, she was free!

The Freedom Keys to Forgiveness

Let me reiterate the essential keys to freedom you can use when helping yourself or someone else get free from the bondage of pain:

- Connect with the trauma instead of running from it.
- Verbalize (privately or with a trusted counselor) how the violator caused you to feel.
- Ask the Holy Spirit how He views the violator, and experience His compassion for the person. Then pray a prayer of forgiveness for the violator.

These are the fundamental components of experiencing the Father heart of God in the midst of a painful situation.

Unforgiveness is a relentless taskmaster that guards the dungeon of past offenses. Forgiveness is a choice, but it is not an option for anyone who wants to live a joy-filled life. It is important to remember that forgiveness is an act of the will, not an act of the emotions. You cannot measure the depth of your forgiveness by your feelings. When Jesus forgave us for all our sins, He gave us the power to forgive everybody who has wronged us. We know when we have truly forgiven, because we no longer want the one who has wronged us to be punished.

Forgiveness is a choice, but it is not an option for anyone who wants to live a joy-filled life.

Sometimes forgiveness is like a seed planted in the good soil of your heart. As you water the seed of forgiveness by reminding yourself over and over again that you choose to release from punishment the person or persons who have harmed you, the pain in your soul begins to dissipate. Once you have made the right choices, your wounds stop festering and your heart heals. Although this process may take time, you can be assured that you will fully heal.

REFLECT

1. Have you partnered with guilt and shame? If so, ask the Holy Spirit why you have been keeping shame in your life. (You can refer back to this chapter's section titled "Guilt and Shame" to help you.)

2. Let's uproot shame by asking the Father what He thinks about it, and then by replacing the lie that shame is telling you with what God's truth is. Remember, shame thrives in darkness, so when you expose shame to the light, it begins to lose its power. Over the next few days, it may also be helpful for you to talk to a trusted friend or mentor about the shame you have been experiencing. Again, the more you expose shame, the weaker it gets!

3. Next, take any unforgiveness you may have toward yourself or another person and refer back to the steps for processing pain at the end of chapter 6. Take each trespass one by one and deal with it. (Sometimes this process takes a few months, since you should only process one or two incidents a day because you cannot process well if you are emotionally drained.)

EIGHT

True Love

I climbed into bed, exhausted from the workings of a demanding day, and I quickly fell into a deep sleep and began to dream. In what felt like only moments, I found myself trapped in a room made of glass. It was not long before I realized that this place was like no other place I had ever been before. In a panic I searched for an exit, but there was none.

My anxiety increased as I began beating my fists against the walls of glass, trying to bust through. Then my terror turned to wonder as I realized the walls were solid, yet fluid and alive. As I pushed against them, I began to feel a strong current of emotion flowing through the walls, like what you would feel if you were standing in a river. As I leaned into one wall, the weight of love for the whole world fell so heavily upon me that I dropped to my knees.

It was in this moment that I realized I was caught up in eternity, held there by an unknown force. Overwhelmed by this intense feeling of love for the world, I began to peer deeper into the wall. The farther I looked inside, the more I could see what looked like billions of movies of all kinds. I began to realize what was going on. These were not movies at all, but the lives of people in motion right before my eyes. With my heart pounding, I began to ask questions out loud, not necessarily expecting an answer.

"*How did I get here?*" I shouted.

Instantly, as if the question had been anticipated, a voice answered back, "I brought you here."

The words of the One who answered burned deep into my heart. I had never felt that kind of compassion before. As He spoke, His presence began to encompass me like a thick fog. I could feel holiness radiating through every cell of my body. For the first time in my life I felt pure love, and the weight of the world lifted off me. As I was lying face down, I could sense His excitement building as I connected to His heart, and His thoughts became my thoughts.

> I could feel holiness radiating through every cell of my body. For the first time in my life I felt pure love, and the weight of the world lifted off me.

"I want to show you why I brought you here," He said.

A movie of my life began to run in reverse, right in front of my eyes . . . rewinding past my birth, past my conception and into eternity. As the movie unfolded, I could see myself standing with God in a timeless place . . . before the earth was created. He pointed to me and said, "I knew you here!" Then He fast-forwarded the movie to my conception in my mother's womb. I watched as He carefully formed me. A set of blueprints with my name on it appeared, and I watched as God built one-of-a-kind attributes into me. Talents, abilities, personality and looks were meticulously fashioned in my mother's womb, according to His perfect plan.

Next, He reached into my heart and planted a deep purpose for my being me . . . something that no one else could ever fulfill, a call that only I could accomplish. As I watched Him form me in silence, I realized that each of my attributes was actually a piece of His likeness. People could therefore experience a part of God by observing my life.

When the movie ended, He picked me up, sat me in His lap and held me so tightly. He said, "You're my favorite . . . you've always been my favorite!" His words ran like liquid love through my body, bringing healing to every broken place in me and setting me free.

In His Image

Thousands of years ago, God spoke to the prophet Jeremiah and said, "Before I formed you in the womb I knew you" (Jeremiah 1:5). In Genesis 1:26, God said, "Let us make mankind in our image, in our likeness." Think about that for a second—the most amazing, beautiful Master Craftsman created us in His own image. This is an incredible statement about how we were made! The second thing that is important to know about these verses is that God had our history planned before the beginning of time. If He knew that we were going to be born, then He must have had a plan and a purpose for our lives, because God does not make mistakes.

> We were created by divine design. God is not sitting up in heaven, wondering what He is going to do with all these people who are being born.

The apostle Paul wrote, "In him we were also chosen, having been predestined according to the plan of him who works out everything in conformity with the purpose of his will" (Ephesians 1:11). We were created by divine design. God is not sitting up in heaven, wondering what He is going to do with all these people who are being born.

One of the greatest violations of our relationship with Christ is to misunderstand who we are and how we were made. When we devalue ourselves, we are diminishing the Creator, because we were made in His image. Not only that, but when we receive Christ, He gives us the ability to completely transform our mind from our old, earthly thinking into thinking like the King Himself, which is why the Bible says, "We have the mind of Christ" (1 Corinthians 2:16).

The Truth about Love

Many Christians have been taught exactly the opposite, that they are not valuable and unique. If you remember back to the story of Jody, her greatest problem was that she did not love herself and could not forgive herself. Usually, the hardest person in the world to forgive is ourselves. These two things added together equal the Church becoming a broken-down, arthritic Bride begging for her Husband to come back and save her, instead of a victorious Bride who is bringing heaven to earth.

Most of the world's problems are rooted in self-hatred, because we will never let somebody love us more than we love ourselves. That is why Jesus said, "Love your neighbor as yourself" (Matthew 22:39). If we don't love ourselves, then when somebody else has a deep love for us, the thought of that person rejecting us is incredibly painful. So without even knowing it, instead of risking major rejection, we do things subconsciously to sabotage the relationship in order to protect ourselves.

Another scenario that often plays out when somebody loves us more than we love ourselves is that we become overly dependent (codependent) on that person because we are afraid of him or her leaving us. Then we live our entire life at the mercy of another person, instead of being able to set boundaries and share our most intimate needs, which is true love. That is why Solomon wrote, "Under three things the earth quakes, and under four, it cannot bear up," with the third thing being "an unloved woman when she gets a husband" (Proverbs 30:21, 23 NASB).

The standard with which we love ourselves is also the standard with which we will love others. Without a doubt, if you don't love yourself, the chances of your loving somebody else according to God's standard will be slim to none. You cannot walk around hating who you are, and then, out of the very same vessel, extend life and hope to the people around you. It just does not work that way. Loving yourself according to God's standard is the only way that you will ever have truly happy and healthy relationships.

> Loving yourself according to God's standard is the only way that you will ever have truly happy and healthy relationships.

There are so many different opinions about love and what it is that it feels foolish to go on any further without defining it. Love is not a fleeting emotion that comes and goes with the wind. Nor is it a spark that was created in a combustible moment of euphoria. Love is a choice. Love is sacrifice. Love is boundaries, and yet, love is unconditional.

The most beautiful living model of love that we have ever had on earth is Jesus. He was and is the embodiment of true love. He took care of Himself and His own needs, yet He was powerful, and He gave. He brought the best of Himself to every situation and used it to build the best in others. And finally, He yielded Himself to the whip and to the cross to restore our relationship with the Father.

Jesus said, "Greater love has no one than this: to lay down one's life for one's friends" (John 15:13). His ability to lay down His life and build others up rested in the fact that He first loved Himself. He knew where He came from and what the Father had commissioned Him to do; therefore, He knew how unique He was and what He had to give.

Who Do You Say You Are?

It is not enough just to know what the Scriptures say about you, because your identity does not lie in your head. It is embedded in your heart. Jesus said, "A good man brings good things out of the good stored up in his heart, and an evil man brings evil things out of the evil stored up in his heart. For the mouth speaks what the heart is full of" (Luke 6:45). Who we are and what we believe to be true about ourselves is derived from multiple places—both our head and our heart.

If you are starting out behind the curve, and you are reading this book and saying to yourself, *I don't think I love myself the way I should*, go back and reread my dream about creation at the beginning of this chapter. Recall how God made you and how He sees you. Spend time every day going over these truths until they become yours.

Next, "Take captive every thought to make it obedient to Christ" (2 Corinthians 10:5). Treat every thought that is dangerous to your identity or contrary to what God says about you as a trespasser. These thoughts are evil by nature and are only there to erode your identity. You have permission to tell any thought that does not line up with God's Word to leave your mind.

Now, let's check how you talk to yourself. Studies show that we talk to ourselves at the rate of 150 to 300 words a minute, or nearly 50,000 thoughts per day. Of those thoughts, 70 percent are negative words, and 70 percent of that negative self-talk happens at a subconscious level.

> Treat every thought that is dangerous to your identity or contrary to what God says about you as a trespasser.

Furthermore, 95 percent of what you say to yourself will be repeated will be repeated the next day.

I cannot stress enough how important it is to begin to take control of your thought life, even your subconscious thoughts. If you spend half your day berating yourself with negative trash, it is literally impossible to believe that you are worthy of love. Christians are the worst at this, because we often believe that all we have to do is "name it and proclaim it." Proclamation is good, but it is not a fix-all. Learning how to access your subconscious, negative thoughts and confront them is key. In order to do this, you will have to become self-aware of your moods. Anytime your mood changes from fun and positive to bad, chances are that you had a thought go through your mind at some level that does not line up with what the Lord is saying over you. These thoughts should be treated like enemies and be driven out and replaced by what God says over you. Renewing your mind is a proactive process. The next time you notice a change in your mood, or even a negative craving, take a moment to pause and ask yourself, *Why do I feel this way? What am I saying or believing that is making me feel like this?* In doing so, you will become really good at addressing the thoughts that are running through your mind below the surface by becoming conscious of them. When this process happens, you can effectively address each one head on.

Positive self-talk has to be a huge part of the life of a believer in order for that person to be healthy and whole. Take a look at what happened to you last week and ask yourself how many times you had thoughts in your head that were not from God. Bethel Church's senior pastor, Bill Johnson, says, "We can't allow ourselves to have a thought in our head that is not in His." How many times did you talk to yourself in a destructive way this week?

I often tell people who are struggling with their identity, "You have permission at red traffic lights to catch yourself thinking about how awesome you are!" The religious spirit says, *You're going to drive people into pride!* But the truth is that when we keep in mind that we were born to be amazing because we were modeled after Jesus and created by God Himself, then pride is the last thing we need to worry about. Pride comes most often when we are trying to lift ourselves up because of our insecurity.

Counterfeit Loves

One of love's greatest tragedies is that it has been mistaken for passion. True love is rooted in sacrifice—the laying down and the giving of life. Passion is an emotion that is felt most often in the pursuit and exploration of another. We should not exchange passion for love. Nor should the pursuit of passion ever come before the foundation of love. When relationships are based on passion, emotion determines the depth of the connection, and before you know it, you are hearing statements from married couples like "we just fell out of love." Give me a break! You cannot fall out of love any more than you can fall into love.

> One of love's greatest tragedies is that it has been mistaken for passion. True love is rooted in sacrifice— the laying down and the giving of life.

Love is a choice. When couples make the choice to stop sacrificing and laying down their lives for each other, love goes dormant and the relationships begin to die. Passion is a healthy part of intimate relationships when love is at the core of the covenant. But if a couple uses passion as the glue to bond them together, the relationship will just be a flash fire instead of an eternal flame.

Love's promise is this: You will feel. A heart encased in steel feels nothing. After being deeply wounded by love and its many façades, I knew deep inside that in order to love again, I would have to risk again. But with so many hurtful brands of love in this world, I was tempted to throw away the key to the protective cage that surrounded my heart. If I was going to be able to hold the gates of my heart open, I would have to be watchful for love's many counterfeits. Three main examples of counterfeits are selfish love, no-needs love and drunken love. Let's examine what each of these three looks like, which will help us avoid them and others like them.

Selfish Love

The first counterfeit is selfish love. This kind of "love" gives only for the purpose of getting back. It is usually short-lived, leaving behind flash fires and burned bridges.

Selfish love is neatly packed in sweet talk and smooth moves, wooing its victim to vulnerability before dealing the fatal blow.

The telltale sign of selfish love lies in its inability to sacrifice and serve another. When you find yourself in a situation with someone who is unwilling to meet anyone else's needs besides his or her own, feel free to tuck your tail and run!

No-Needs Love

Another counterfeit is "selfless" love, which sounds like a good thing until you think about it in the context of the someone who does not express any of his or her needs. Selfless love of this kind gives to anyone who demands something of it, with the hope of one day being able to fill the bottomless pit in the heart of the one who is "loving" others in this way. People who extend this kind of no-needs love have their identity wrapped up in the fact that they are the blood that keeps the leeches alive.

Powerless people who pretend to have no needs usually offer this kind of love. But without sharing of their own needs, love between them and another person is never whole.

In these kinds of relationships, there is only one powerful person, and it is not the no-needs lover. But the underlying fear in such a "selfless" heart is that if it has needs of its own and shares them, it will be left all alone.

Drunken Love

The third counterfeit of love is drunken love (also known as blind love). Drunken love is fueled purely by an intoxicated state of emotions, usually brought on by desperation and fear. This dangerous love pushes past all boundaries, failing to yield at warning signs, in pursuit of a fix.

Drunken love is sure to leave you in a pile of sober regret, with little or nothing gained. You can usually tell when you are in this situation, because your community around you is screaming, *"Danger!"* But the drunken lover justifies his or her intoxication with clichés like "nobody understands me." Anytime you are using this justification to stay in a relationship, you are in deep water!

My Life Now

When my marriage crashed, I learned a lot about myself. In the vulnerability of desiring to truly love others, I am continually urged to grow. Every relationship stretches me, and with each mistake or hurt, I have to make a choice to learn instead of run. Love is risky business, and there are no guarantees when it comes to trusting another person. My questions abound as the plow of the relational process continually turns over the soil of my heart. I must understand how to love, while using discernment regarding love's true nature. Love without a standard is not love at all. It is just brokenness trying to find a home.

> Love without a standard is not love at all. It is just brokenness trying to find a home.

There are many faces that mask themselves as true love, but whenever I have experienced their fruit, I have found that they lack the attributes of all that love encompasses. Those who partake of these false loves think they have tasted the real thing, but they are left hurting. In order to find true love, I had to know its attributes. In 1 Corinthians 13:4–7, Paul beautifully describes true love's characteristics:

Love is patient, love is kind. It does not envy, it does not boast, it is not proud. It does not dishonor others, it is not self-seeking, it is not easily angered, it keeps no record of wrongs. Love does not delight in evil but rejoices with the truth. It always protects, always trusts, always hopes, always perseveres.

Love is freedom. Love is wholeness. Love is honoring. As I traversed down love's path again, I was reminded of this truth that I am the only one who has the power to decide what type of relationship I will be involved in. I control my standard.

Love is not love unless it costs me something. Love is not love unless it seeks only the highest good of the other person. Love is not love unless it leads to freedom.

Having been so wounded in a relationship and now having come out on the other side, I can see and appreciate true love's amazing attributes. I realize now that God loves me unconditionally. After going through what felt like the end of my life, I recognize that although I was not perfect myself, it was not my choices that nearly killed me, but the choices of another. We both had some shortcomings, but regardless of her issues and her abuse of our relationship, I never lost my love for her or my hope for her to be whole. If I can go through that and love her in spite of all that has happened, how much more does God love me? After all, I am the person who put Him on the cross and broke Him open with the whip.

> Love is not love unless it seeks only the highest good of the other person. Love is not love unless it leads to freedom.

REFLECT

1. Take a look at the relationships in your life for a moment. Do they meet the 1 Corinthians 13 standard? If not, it is time to set some boundaries in order to create healthy, loving relationships. If you are not sure how to do that, dive into the book I mentioned at the end of chapter 2, *Boundaries* by Dr. John Townsend and Dr. Henry Cloud.

2. Do you love yourself as God loves you, or do you need to apply repentance to the way you have seen yourself? Remember that love without a standard is not love at all. It is just brokenness trying to find a home. By establishing good boundaries and setting a standard for yourself, you are saying "I'm valuable!"

3. Reflect on your inner world and thought life. Who do you tell yourself you are? Is your self-talk positive or negative?

4. If your thoughts are not lining up with what God says about you, begin the process of taking them captive. You literally will have to catch yourself when you are having negative thoughts and immediately address them, changing your inner dialogue about yourself.

NINE

Red Flags

So many factors play into being an emotionally healthy person and living whole in relationship with others. *Peace* is one of those factors that you just cannot leave home without.

Many times in my life I have found myself in these epic battles, fighting to possess my own peace. These wars were not announced by the sound of a trumpet to warn me of the presence of an opposing enemy, nor were there soldiers standing on a battlefield in plain sight, holding shields and spears. The battlefield was in my mind, and the opponents were the deceptive lies that had crept in undetected.

Since you are among the living, I am sure you have experienced what I am talking about. These opponents that we fight manifest themselves in the form of insecurity, anger, loneliness, rejection, self-pity, frustration and so on. And although these feelings are not necessarily evil in themselves, if left unattended, they will become as destructive as the devil himself.

One of the most important things to know about these feelings is that they need immediate attention because they have so much influence over us. I refer to these feelings as "red flags." Every red flag, whether it is loneliness or insecurity or anything else, leaves you extremely vulnerable to the violation of yourself or another emotionally. It is also important to know that at the end or beginning of a relationship, you will be most susceptible to these red flags.

> One of the most important things to know about "red flag" feelings is that they need immediate attention because they have so much influence over us.

A while back, I woke up at 7:00 a.m. to find that my brain had already been up and processing for quite some time. As I lay in bed, thoughts of insecurity rolled through my mind one by one, making themselves known to me. For a second, I thought about just pushing them aside and going back to sleep, hoping they would somehow disappear. But the longer I lay there, the more I began to realize that these saboteurs were not going to leave peacefully. Insecurity slowly began to take over my entire soul, to the point that it became all I could think about. Realizing this was not my normal state of mind, I had to make a decision: try to ignore it, or battle it out.

I decided that leaving the house with a starving heart and no peace was probably a really bad idea. And since I had the day off, I decided to spend the better part of three hours lying in my bed, battling it out, knowing that the consequences of walking around feeling insecure are costly. Here is why: During this season in my life, my job was to help oversee 800 Bethel school of ministry students and 10 pastors, plus pastoring 65 students of my own. Most of my duties as a pastor and an overseer of the school landed me in an office, counseling young students through their issues. If I walk into a room with a hurting student and am feeling needy and insecure myself, I am taking a very high risk of spilling my insecurity onto the student sitting across from me and infecting that person with something he or she did not walk in with. Even if I don't necessarily negatively affect someone else's peace of mind with my feelings, if I somehow feel better about myself or less insecure because of what he or she says about me, then I have become a slave to the praise of man, and I will always be at its mercy.

Small Flames Become Forest Fires

Throughout this book, I have given you multiple examples of people who have damaged themselves or someone else. Each of those violations did not originally start as an infringement; rather, it began as a small spark that was left unattended and eventually grew into a forest fire of damage to others.

A great example of this, although admittedly a harsh one, is the life of Ted Bundy. Bundy was one of the most feared, cold-blooded serial killers of our time. But he did not start as a hardened soul looking for blood. He began as a young man who, at the age of thirteen, got addicted to pornography. His addiction to soft porn dramatically increased as the years went on. Soon he craved more explicit and violent scenes, which eventually led him deeper into his addiction, until he finally became the Ted Bundy we all know about.

I realize his story is an off-the-charts example of what happens with something that starts small, but the truth is that if Ted Bundy had taken care of the need he had in his heart at the age of thirteen, when it was just a spark, it would have forever changed the lives of many people, including his own. I realize that someone who is thirteen probably does not have the emotional intelligence to know how to figure out all the dynamics of what is going on inside and out, and that is why it is so important for parents and mentors to create a culture where it is normal for kids to be open and honest and even ask the hard questions of life. Although Bundy was not getting what he needed from his immediate family, young people often have the option somehow to seek help outside their family system, whether from a school counselor, a doctor, a youth group pastor or a trusted family friend. But because he failed to find out what he needed and get help (even later in his life, when he was more emotionally mature), the spark of perversion and the need for significance grew into a rage that cost many people their lives.

Dating is a less dramatic example of how unhealthy people can create dysfunctional relationships. In a dating relationship, it is really common for insecurity to drive the relationship faster than it should go, causing both parties involved to get to a place of intimacy without building the foundation of trust. No one likes to feel insecure in a relationship, but the lie is, "If we would just get to the point in this relationship where he/she is fully committed, then my insecurity would be gone." The intimacy pace therefore picks up, and boundaries get crossed. Two years down the road, you are married and discover that the foundation of trust is missing, so you are left scrambling to find your legs in the relationship.

On the flip side, if you know you are feeling insecure in a relationship and you take the time to deal with that insecurity, then both of you are protected. Instead of fear as the driving force of your relationship, your motivation for going deeper is built on trust.

> If you know you are feeling insecure in a relationship and you take the time to deal with that insecurity, then both of you are protected.

I could literally give you a hundred examples of things that start small and work their way into massive issues. But the most important thing I want you to learn here is that any red flag—whether insecurity, loneliness, frustration, self-hatred, anger or the like—that goes unheeded and unchecked will eventually grow into something massive. It may not be today or tomorrow, but it is much like a sliver under your skin. Left unattended, that sliver will begin to fester and will grow an infection until it is so painful that you don't want anyone to touch it. But until you remove the sliver, the infection will continue to get worse.

The Importance of Self-Awareness

Every person has a set of needs that, if unmet, will eventually lead to some kind of pain. Many people are extremely detached from what they really think, feel and need. The problem with this is that we humans are designed to get our needs met, regardless of whether or not we are conscious of them. And without being cognizant of what we really need, the chances of getting our needs met in a healthy way lessen dramatically, the more unaware we are of them.

The process of becoming conscious of what you think, feel and need is called becoming "self-aware." Becoming self-aware is one of the greatest defenses we have. Without this ability, we walk through a battlefield without armor, and with a large bull's-eye drawn on our chest. Then it is only a matter of time before we get shot through the heart by a poor decision we did not even see coming.

The process of becoming self-aware is not rocket science, but it is a practice that requires daily attendance and attention. There are actually several ways to become good at the skill of knowing what is going on in your heart. The ways I want to look at here are paying attention to how you feel, exploring the benefits of journaling, taking a personality test and identifying your greatest unmet need. But the first step, of course, is to recognize that you have needs that will require you to take some kind of action. Once you acknowledge that, follow it up with these next steps.

> Without self-awareness, we walk through a battlefield without armor, and with a large bull's-eye drawn on our chest.

Pay Attention to How You Feel

One of the best ways you can help yourself find out what you need is by paying attention to how you feel. For example, if you are feeling angry, somewhere inside you there is a need trying to be met. Anger, for example, can stem from feeling powerless and out of control. If you are feeling angry, stop for a second and go back to the place that triggered that feeling.

A person can feel angry for many reasons, but if you go back to where your anger began, you will find the answer to why you feel that way. You may not be able to solve the main problem that brought about the anger, but you can decide what you are going to do with your feelings.

Paul said, "In your anger do not sin" (Ephesians 4:26), which means that there is no shame in feeling frustration, insecurity or anger. It is what we do with our feelings that matters in life.

Explore the Benefit of Journaling

Another great way to find out what you need is to spend time alone, writing in a journal without editing your thoughts. I often begin journaling not even knowing how I am feeling or why I am feeling a certain way. By the time I am done writing out my thoughts and what happened in my day, however, I am able to figure out where I am at and why.

In the same way, sitting down with a really close friend and talking through your thoughts and emotions can be an excellent way to figure out what you need and what is going on inside you.

Take a Personality Test

Another factor that plays heavily into the red flags of your life is your personality type. All of us have a personality type with its own set of strengths and weaknesses. By learning what personality traits you possess, you can discover what fears you are prone to and what you tend to need in order to feel healthy and secure. Understanding your possible needs and fears will allow you to pay closer attention to those areas of your life.

When you develop a culture around you that takes into account your natural tendencies, you tend to live a more healthy and happy life. For example, are you more energized by working in the spotlight or working behind the scenes? That trait should factor into the work environment you choose.

One of the easiest ways to discover your strengths and weaknesses is to take a test like the DISC personality test (which measures Dominance, Influence, Steadiness and Compliance factors) or the Myers-Briggs Type Indicator test. These tests are designed to help you find out what personality type you are, which will aid you in developing a healthy environment internally and externally.

Identify Your Greatest Unmet Need

A great way to become more self-aware is to discover your greatest area of pain. For example, if your life has been riddled with rejection, then you know without a doubt that rejection waves a red flag at you. When you are feeling rejected and are not self-aware, you can easily slip back into an old pattern of isolation that takes you down.

In the midst of the darkest days of my ex-wife's betrayal, I discovered that my greatest red flags were insecurity and loneliness. In one day, I went from being a husband married to a beautiful wife, to waking up in my bed alone. Some mornings, waking up alone felt like a cruel game love had played on me. With my wandering mind, I could picture him and her lying together in each other's arms in the comfort of their own home. And although that may have been real, the truth is that before I even got out of bed on a morning like that, I had some pretty major emotional needs that had to be taken care of in order for me to be okay.

Insecurity and loneliness for a guy in my shoes is par for the course; it is even to be expected. It would have been the epitome of foolishness for me to remain unaware of the presence of these emotions. But I quickly learned that loneliness and insecurity were no friends of mine, and anytime they showed their face on my property, I drove them out with a vengeance.

How to Deal with Each Red Flag

We don't get to decide who comes to our door, but we do have a choice about whether or not we let them in. We have to appoint ourselves as the keeper of our lives and the protector of our hearts. We choose our moods, actions and belief systems; therefore, we are powerful enough to change them!

As a leader of a men's sexual purity group, I have discovered that most people's setbacks are the fruit of not recognizing the small spark of hurt until it becomes a forest fire. For many, the cycle of raging out of control has been part of their entire life up to the point that they find themselves in trouble because of their inability to figure out what they need and get it met in a healthy way. You have to have a plan for each red flag you deal with in life.

When I was in the dark valley of my own circumstances, I would wake up each morning and ask myself out loud, "How am I doing? What do I need? Am I hurting . . . or is my heart doing good?" I found out that just taking a little bit of time to know myself every morning made me feel valuable. Usually, if something was off, even just a little bit, I could take care of it quickly because I kept short accounts with myself. Whenever I could not drive away the afflicting feelings quickly, I knew it was time for war. I had already made up my mind that leaving my house with any type of red flag waving from my soul was a really bad idea.

> You have to have a plan for each red flag you deal with in life.

There are probably hundreds of ways to defeat feelings of insecurity, loneliness or hopelessness. But before you can overcome these enemies, you have to understand the root issues of your heart, as we talked about earlier in the book. There is a huge difference between *I'm feeling insecure because of something that just happened in the moment* and *I'm feeling insecure because I don't know that God is my Father.* These two issues are worlds apart and require different kinds of attention.

Ultimately, the way to get rid of red flags that are the offspring of someone else's actions is to figure out what we need and get that need met accordingly. When I would wake up feeling incredibly insecure, I would spend hours lying in bed, talking to God and journaling what He says about me and how He sees me. If that did not take care of the issue completely, then I would call my dad and get some more help.

Insecurity, fear, hopelessness, depression and self-hatred are all rooted in lies. The Bible tells us that when Timothy was struggling with fear, his spiritual father, Paul, wrote these words to him: "God has not given us a spirit of fear, but of power and of love and of a sound mind" (2 Timothy 1:7 NKJV). The greatest trump cards we have in our pocket at all times are the power of the Holy Spirit and the Word of God. The Spirit's power transforms our fears into peace, and God's Word uproots the lies that get planted in our hearts.

You Can Control Only Yourself

The book of Galatians teaches us that self-control is a fruit of the Holy Spirit's involvement in our lives (see Galatians 5:22–23). In this life there are a lot of things we need and want that won't get taken care of because we have no control over the world around us. If we have any other belief system besides the one that says, "I'm in control of only myself," we are living in deception. The only person on the entire planet that you can control in a healthy way is yourself. You can share your feelings and your needs with other people around you, but it is their choice whether or not they take care of those needs for you. This can be an incredibly painful reality, one that many kids experience all around the world, as Ted Bundy did. With that in mind, you have to learn how to be a powerful person regardless of what anyone else in your world does.

Practically, this means that if you are in a place of pain because of the world and the people around you, it is your responsibility to take ownership of what is going on inside you and address the issue. As a pastor, I have helped hundreds of kids and young adults navigate through bad living situations, conflicts with parents and even abusive situations because they personally took ownership

> The only person on the entire planet that you can control in a healthy way is yourself.

and asked for help from an outside source that was safe and willing. The same people could easily have given in to the lie that they were powerless and could have continued to live in destructive environments, but they asked for help instead.

People with a victim mentality see through a lens that shows them this view: *The world is against me. Everyone else gets what I should have. I'm always the one who is left out.* You will know right away if you have a victim mentality because these thoughts will go through your mind on a regular basis. Victims feel as though their circumstances are everyone else's fault. They think that if people would just do things differently or treat them another way, life would be good.

The truth is that when you embrace this mentality, you are the one with the problem. The good news is that if you are the problem, you can fix yourself (but not anyone else) with the help of God.

You Can Think Yourself to Freedom

Paul wrote to the believers in Rome, "Do not be conformed to this world, but be transformed by the renewing of your mind" (Romans 12:2 NKJV). These Roman believers were former polytheists (they worshiped many gods); therefore, conforming to the thought patterns of their world would have meant that they were embracing Roman mythology. Paul taught them that they proactively needed to change the way they thought. Sometimes we all need a good brainwashing with the Word of God (see Ephesians 5:26).

It is scientifically proven that our habits and thought patterns actually cut neurotransmitter grooves, or paths, in our brain. Our core belief system builds freeways that facilitate our thoughts along these pathways. Think about it as a path that has been cut through a dense forest. This path or pattern of thinking is what we have been driving on our entire life. When we make a conscious decision to change the way we think, all we have really done is put a *No Trespassing* sign on that path. Here is where the change process begins: We have to cut a new thought path into our brains that leads to wholeness. Just like sawing through a thick forest, cutting a fresh path is hard work. If we are not careful, we will become blind to the *No Trespassing* signs placed at the freeway entrances of our old patterns of thinking, and we will wind up traveling back down that same dysfunctional and destructive road again because it is so familiar and much easier.

When you are in a lot of pain, you are highly motivated to change. At first, you will do almost anything you are asked to do in order to rid yourself of your current status. But as time goes on and the pain lessens, the motivation to become well typically fades with the pain. One antidote that helps break this pattern is to begin setting attainable goals. These goals will

> We have to cut a new thought path into our brains that leads to wholeness. Just like sawing through a thick forest, cutting a fresh path is hard work.

help motivate you long after your pain is gone. Wisdom says that you should look at your life from the end and work backward. You should not be afraid to take a moment, sit down at the edge of your grave and think about your life. What do you want to be known as? What do you want God to say about you? What is going to be most important to you when you are lying on your deathbed? The answers to these questions should be the motivators of your life.

Pain is a very poor motivator and an even worse counselor. You can no more guide your life with pain than you can navigate a raging sea with a broken compass. It is vision for the future that is your life's compass. By following vision, you will continue to cut through the forest of your mind to create a pathway to freedom long after the pain is gone. A life lived in this fashion is a life that will be remembered for good.

1. What are some of your "red flag" feelings or emotions? Write down each one that you can identify.

2. As we learned in this chapter, we have to have a plan for each red flag we deal with in life, and we need to deal with the red flags right away because they can have so much influence over us. Create a plan for each of your red flags that may pop up unexpectedly during the day. It may be helpful to talk to a friend or therapist about what to do when you feel "triggered."

3. Is there a common emotion/red flag you always tend to experience? If so, what is it? Deep down, what do you think the true need is behind it? What do you need to do in order to meet that need?

4. Is there someone in your life who can help you identify your needs and get them met in a healthy way? Sometimes it may be necessary to seek professional help such as a life coach or counselor.

5. How do you become a more powerful person regardless of what anyone else in your world does?

TEN

Into Me You See

Not too long ago, I had a young man come to me for help. This particular guy grew up in our church, so I have known him for some time. But up until this day, all I really knew of him was what I could see from the outside. John came into my office that day somber, as if someone had drained the hope right out of him. It only took a few words from his mouth for me to see why. He began to share the story of his recent affair, recalling the shame of losing his wife and the torment of his last few months.

As John was sharing his story with me, the thought kept running through my mind, *Why would John cheat on his wife, when he has been married to her only for a matter of months? What would cause him to do that?* As I began to question him, things became clearer to me. On the outside, John was a fine gentleman who had been in church his whole life. But on the inside, John was a dungeon full of tormenting dragons.

John's early childhood memories were riddled with searing pain. His dad used to tie his boys up to trees and beat them with rubber hoses to teach them a lesson. John's dad was a cold, unaffectionate man who taught his sons that "true love" came in the form of punishment. There was nothing John could ever do that was good enough for his dad, and no way for John to hear the words "I love you."

> On the outside, John was a fine gentleman who had been in church his whole life. But on the inside, John was a dungeon full of tormenting dragons.

Shortly into his teenage years, John found the Lord through going to youth group. Instead of this easing the pain, however, in some ways it magnified it. Think about it: There John is at youth group, a young teen dying on the inside for affection. And there he is, amongst a group of kids who all seem to have what he so desperately needs. It is not too long before John realizes that if these kids find out that he is a dungeon on the inside, they will do what his father did—reject him. Unwilling to risk rejection, John learns the fine craft of hiding. He shows many faces to many people, but none of them are real. They are all façades of who he would really like to be, but his many faces are creations of his own imagination.

Time passes by and the pain continues to grow, fueled by the absence of love and the realization that people don't really love him—they love his façade. Unable to make the pain go away on his own, John begins to medicate himself with pornography, hoping somehow to fill that place of intimacy that has never been filled before. But the pain is like a festering wound that won't stop, and now the dungeon is even darker, and the dragons have sunk their accusations deep into his heart. He now knows himself only as a violator of himself and of women.

John continues down this road all the way through his teenage years, until he finally meets his wife in his early twenties. At first, everything is great. The marriage seems like exactly what he has always wanted. He has spent his entire life trying to find someone who would really love him, whom he could really love, and now he has done it! He has found her! How could this possibly go wrong?

John and his wife do not even celebrate a single anniversary before the dragons begin to remind him that she does not know who he really is. After all, he puts on many faces, and all of them are frauds. His fear of ever being found out and rejected is compounded by the fact that the woman he married is a gem. *If she ever finds out who I really am, she won't love me anymore—she never would have loved me in the first place*, he often tells himself.

The pressure continues to build inside John as the days go on and the dragons keep whispering their deceit in his ears. All the while, he continues to retreat farther inside himself, trying to bury who he really is. The fuse has been lit in his relationship, and it is only a matter of time before the resulting lack of intimacy and his constant façade blow the marriage into a thousand pieces. Afterward, alone with his negative thoughts and starving for affection, he goes back to the only place where he has ever found the comfort before; he finds another woman just as broken and hidden as he is himself, and the rest is history.

The Sins of Our Fathers

What John never realized is that the sins of our fathers are not passed down through a hereditary disease; rather, they are passed down by our agreement with our fathers' faulty belief systems. John had never broken away from what his father had taught him growing up. He had clung so tightly to the faulty belief system passed down to him through the beatings and his father's abuse of "love" that it had finally cost him everything. John's dad had taught him how to hide from the world, and he had shown him that the only way to get his needs met was on his own. His father had also proven to his boys that showing vulnerability would only cause them pain—the kind you don't recover from.

> The sins of our fathers are not passed down through a hereditary disease; rather, they are passed down by our agreement with our fathers' faulty belief systems.

The truth about John is that the very thing that he was hiding, Jesus had already taken care of for him. Oftentimes,

I hear Christians say, "If I'm a new creation as Scripture says, then why am I still dealing with the same old stuff?" Scripture does tell us we are new creations in 2 Corinthians 5:17–21, but in Matthew 11:28 Jesus also says, "Come to me, all you who are weary and burdened, and I will give you rest." In essence, God is saying, "Come to Me *as you are*, and I'll meet you there."

This is where the whole thing gets a little tricky. If you take a step back and look at what Christ is saying, you can see that His heart is to make you whole, not to have you come to Him all put together already! I find that most believers who are stuck in their sin have come to Christ the same way that they came to the world—hiding behind their façade and playing Church. Their intentions are good, but they don't understand that Christ is the way out. He is not looking for you to find a way out without Him. The truth is that you actually need Him in order to be victorious.

But the problem lies in this: If you are going to get free, then you have to come to Christ *as you are*. At first glance it does not sound like a big deal, but when you take a look at where Christ is, the feeling becomes a bit more daunting. Ephesians 5:8–14 says,

> For you were once darkness, but now you are light in the Lord. Live as children of light (for the fruit of the light consists in all goodness, righteousness and truth) and find out what pleases the Lord. Have nothing to do with the fruitless deeds of darkness, but rather expose them.

It is shameful even to mention what the disobedient do in secret. But everything exposed by the light becomes visible—and everything that is illuminated becomes a light. This is why it is said:

"Wake up, sleeper, rise from the dead, and Christ will shine on you."

This is a powerful passage because Paul is not talking to unbelievers, but rather is talking to a church full of believers. He is reminding them not to hide, but to bring everything into the light, because it is only in the light that we are free. If these words are true, then what happens when we come to Christ but hide pieces of ourselves in the dark? This is the part John never took hold of. He came to Christ desperate, wanting to feel something he had never felt before, wanting to be free and loved. To be completely honest, in a lot of ways he was freer than he had ever been before, and he was saved. But he had only opened up certain parts of his heart to the Lord, keeping deep inside the dragons that haunted him because of the faulty belief system he had "inherited" from his father. The parts of his heart that he had opened up had become free and whole, but there was an entire world of darkness that the Lord did not have access to heal.

> Paul is not talking to unbelievers, but rather is talking to a church full of believers. He is reminding them not to hide, but to bring everything into the light, because it is only in the light that we are free.

In previous chapters, we talked about the effects that shame has over us. Just as shame holds a person bound, the fear of rejection does likewise. If you never come to Christ as you are, then you never feel Him love you as you are. And if you never feel the unconditional acceptance of Christ's love when you are in the midst of the trash, then you will always feel as though you have to perform for His love. If you come to Christ as you are, however, and He loves you in the midst of your sin, then through the shining light of the Lord He will make you whole again. The fear of rejection and shame will be broken off you, making you a new creation.

Adam and Eve

Most of us know the story of Adam and Eve and the cunning serpent who introduced sin into the world. The basic story goes like this: It starts with God creating Adam first. It was not long, however, before God realized that it was not good for man to be alone. The interesting part about this whole scenario is that Adam was not alone; he had God walking with him every day, and he also was amongst the animals. But Adam had no one to help him rule the earth, and he had no one to share his life with.

I should stop here and say that there is a place in your life that only God can fill, but there is also a place in your life that only other people can fill. Without that, you may feel all alone. Getting back to the story, however, God in all His wisdom creates a woman from a rib of Adam's, making it possible for him to meet all his relational needs.

Adam and Eve enjoyed a life of ease. They walked with the Lord in the cool of the day, and I imagine at twilight they laid in the grass and enjoyed the stars above. But unfortunately, this life of luxury did not last long. The devil worked his deception, and Adam and Eve both wound up eating the only fruit out of the whole Garden that God said they could not eat.

> There is a place in your life that only God can fill, but there is also a place in your life that only other people can fill.

To make a long story short, Adam and Eve both realized for the first time that they were naked, and they hid from the Lord and covered themselves with leaves. And shortly thereafter, they were removed from the Garden and left to fend for themselves out in the wild world beyond Eden. I just want to bring a few things to light from this story. When sin is introduced into our lives, we begin to hide, as Adam and Eve did. Once sin takes root, it begins to damage the most important part of our lives, our intimacy with God and other people. The day that Adam and Eve fell was the first day that they no longer felt accepted just as they were, naked.

The sin that crept in after the Fall severely damaged the level of intimacy between the Creator and His children. And this has been the case ever since. For the last 2,000-plus years, the greatest attack on humankind has been designed to isolate and choke out the intimacy in our lives. We were designed with intimacy in mind—the kind of intimacy between God and us, and between other people and us, that allows us to share a closeness built on trust. The kind of intimacy that allows us to say "Into me you see." The kind where we see into each other's hearts.

Such intimacy is just the opposite of the modern parable I started with in chapter 5, of the frozen heart that had locked itself away in a cold, dark, self-made prison of ice. Sin and sorrow can cause us to freeze up and want to hide, but when we come to Christ just as we are, and we let His light shine on our dark places, everything changes. When we accept the invitation in Ephesians 5:14, "Wake up, sleeper, rise from the dead, and Christ will shine on you," we can live again and become whole.

1. How do you see intimacy and why? How does the phrase "into me you see" change your perspective on it?

2. Did you adopt any faulty belief systems from your parents that have caused "the sins of our fathers" to become an issue in your life? Ask the Holy Spirit to free you from any faulty beliefs and replace them with His truths to live by.

3. Is there anything about yourself that you hide because you feel as though if people knew about it, they would not love you? Ask God what He has to say about this area, or any others like it. Remember to come to Him *as you are*, and then let Him take it from there.

4. The way to true intimacy takes courage. Create some daily goals to grow connection with others in your life. Some people may need to share their story with someone they trust. Others may need to invite feedback from wise counselors or friends. What do you need to do differently tomorrow to open up a bit more?

ELEVEN

A New Standard

Kris Vallotton

If I'm honest with myself, there is something inside me (actually, inside each of us) that says, *A person who messes up deserves to be punished!* One of the problems with this way of thinking is that we begin to define people by their mistakes instead of by their created origin. A person who lies becomes a liar. A person who gets drunk is labeled an alcoholic. Whores, adulterers, pornographers and murderers are all alias names we give to people when we view them through their sin instead of through the lens of God's divine design.

The second that we connect people's sin with their identity, or label people by their worst action, we feel justified in punishing them. For example, in the Church I have often heard someone refer to a person as a "Jezebel" or a "Judas." The moment we name somebody after an enemy, we no longer want to reconcile with that person. Instead, we are positioning ourselves to excommunicate him or her from our relational circle. We leave the bonds of love at home, and we bring the weapons of warfare to the friendship banquet.

Creating a Culture of Reward

Identifying people by their failures creates a culture where rules replace relationship, and where justice trumps love. It becomes more important to be right than to be together. If you examine most of our social systems, you will find structures that are set up to punish people. We have become a rule-based society instead of a love-based one. *Redemption*, *reconciliation* and *reward* are often hollow words in our culture. For example, when you see a police car following you, by nature you look down at your speedometer to make sure you are not speeding, because you understand that the officer is commissioned to find you doing something wrong, not something right.

> If you examine most of our social systems, you will find structures that are set up to punish people. We have become a rule-based society instead of a love-based one.

Can you imagine a world where officials are charged with rewarding people for their accomplishments as their first priority? It might look something like this: You look in your rearview mirror and see a highway patrolman with his red light on behind you. You look down at your speedometer to assure yourself that you are driving well below the speed limit. An excitement begins to build in you as you make your way over to the shoulder of the freeway.

The officer walks up to your driver's window, smiling. He says, "I've been following you for several miles and have noticed how politely and safely you are driving. Here are two tickets to the Super Bowl. I hope you have a great time."

This example may sound crazy, but welcome to Kingdom thinking. When we received Christ, we were transferred out of the kingdom of darkness and into the Kingdom of God. We left the culture of punishment behind and moved into the New World of reward. The Lord reiterated this truth over and over again in the Bible. In fact, the last chapter closes with Jesus saying, "Behold, I am coming quickly, and My reward is with Me, to render to every man according to what he has done" (Revelation 22:12 NASB).

What about Redemption?

The religious spirit wants to protect rules rather than relationships. The New Testament tells us that the Pharisees constantly scolded Jesus for breaking rules. When

He would heal somebody on the Sabbath day, the Pharisees would get all pushed out of shape about it. Then Jesus would remind them, "The Sabbath was made for man, and not man for the Sabbath" (Mark 2:27 NASB).

Rules, laws and policies should always serve the redemptive purposes of God. Whenever societies require people to serve the rules above serving the people, crucifixion is always the outcome. Our American prison system in many ways has become an example of a culture of punishment, and not of redemption. The goal of much of our justice system is to punish criminals rather than rehabilitate them.

Let me make it clear here that when people cannot control themselves internally, society is obligated to control them externally so that society itself can remain healthy and safe. But when we make it our job to punish people for their sins, we lose sight of society's primary role of redeeming and restoring people. If we believe that sinners need to be punished rather than redeemed, and that sin requires separation, we create a dysfunctional civilization.

> When we make it our job to punish people for their sins, we lose sight of society's primary role of redeeming and restoring people.

Of course, we always create structures of punishment in the absence of an awareness of our own need for God's redemption and forgiveness. It seems funny to me how people in need of so much mercy can be so judgmental.

Rebuilding Trust

One of the greatest challenges in building a redemptive society is the question of how we actually help people rebuild trust and restore relationships. We are all aware that without a supernatural intervention from God, change is often a difficult process that requires unknown amounts of time and patience. We certainly cannot change somebody else, but we can create an environment that fosters the redemptive process for people who are in the midst of their metamorphosis.

One man I know quite well is a great example of someone who brought sin into his houseful of kids through a decades-long addiction and then had an encounter with God that empowered him to change. As you can imagine, he encountered a lot of resistance from his family, who had desperately wanted him to change, yet afterward found it difficult ever to trust him again.

Because sin cuts so deep, the first reaction that someone encounters on the path to restoration is usually based in fear. For so long, this family had been trying to keep this husband and father's toxic behavior from completely destroying them. Each family member had built up his or her own system of defense against him, depending on the level of pain he had caused. Before he changed, he had put his family members in a position where they had to defend themselves somehow in order to survive in the environment he had created.

Here is where it gets tricky: This man is no longer living in sin and creating pain in his environment. But because he did it for so long and hurt his wife and children so deeply, their old way of seeing him is seared into their brains. Understandably, over time his wife became the punisher, responsible for condemning his every sin, and his kids became distant. But he is no longer the man they still see him as. So now what is he going to do? His wife is still playing the role of the punisher, and his kids are still distant, regardless of his change of heart and full repentance.

These are the circumstances in which most people decide that changing is too hard, so they fall back into the comfort of their old roles. For all his good changes, this man felt powerless and started becoming numb to the effects of his punisher, while his wife dished out her victim spirit by the shovelful. If he is ever going to change that dynamic between them, he will have to learn to love and forgive himself, and he will have to reset the standard for himself in the home. We will look at how to accomplish that kind of reset in a minute, but first let's take a look at God's view of restoration, which sets the standard for our own.

God's View of Restoration

In the book of 2 Samuel, chapters 11–12, we find one of the most incredible displays of God's character in the midst of man's failure. We love to think about the heroic stories of King David, who killed a lion and a bear without a weapon, and who slew a giant with just a slingshot and a pebble. David is the envy of every young man. Yet this man after God's own heart committed adultery and murdered his friend!

If you are unfamiliar with the story, it goes something like this: In a time when kings were supposed to go to war, David stayed home. That was his first big mistake. *The safest place in the world for us to be is in God's will.* We are more secure on a battlefield with God than in a fortified palace by ourselves.

Nevertheless, King David sits home while his men are out on the battlefield, and when he decides one night to take a leisurely stroll up on his roof patio, he finds himself looking down upon a woman taking a bath below. In his boredom, he sends messengers to summon the woman to come to him. That night, romance fills the air as David has sex with one of his best friend's wives.

Before long, Bathsheba brings David news that she is pregnant, and David's sin is about to be exposed. In a panic, David summons her husband, Uriah, to come home from the battlefield immediately. David knows that if Uriah does not have sex with his wife, David's own adulterous relationship with her will be discovered.

To make a long story short, Uriah comes back from the battlefield, and in loyalty to his men, who are also away from their families and are sleeping on the hard ground at night, he refuses to go sleep with his wife, regardless of all of King David's efforts to get him to go home. Frustrated and scared, King David sends Uriah back to the battlefield, carrying his own death warrant—a letter from David to

Joab, Uriah's commander, with instructions to send Uriah to the front lines and then retreat from him so he would be killed.

An honorable, mighty man falls that day on the battle-field of sin. When Bathsheba hears the news of her husband's death, she mourns for days. Afterward, she marries the king and moves into the palace. I am sure David was wishing none of this had happened. But the bad news continues and Bathsheba miscarries their first child. After mourning the child's death, David sleeps with her again and she gives birth to the next king. God instructs them to name him Solomon.

This story demonstrates the redemptive nature of God. David's life is a picture of tragedy and triumph. Yet for me, the most beautiful part of the story is God's incred-ible ability to take a horrible situation and bring about His royal purposes. Solomon, one of the greatest kings in Israel's history, was born to parents who had committed adultery and to a father who had committed murder. But even more profound, King David is listed as a father of Jesus Christ (meaning in the line of Christ's direct fore-bears; see Matthew 1:1; 9:27; 20:30; Mark 10:47; 12:35; Luke 18:38; 2 Timothy 2:8; Revelation 22:16).

The life of King David reads like a soap opera, yet within its pages there is hope for everyone who has ever failed miserably and lived in regret. For those of us who, like David, have made destructive choices that have cost other people, we need to remember that we can never fall so far that God cannot find us, or fall so fast that God cannot catch us, or fall so hard that God cannot put us back together again.

And for those of us who are on the receiving end of somebody else's poor choices, this story reveals God's heart toward destructive people. Long after the most merciful among us has thrown in the towel, the Lord is still there, extending His hand of mercy and grace to people like us who don't deserve it.

That does not mean it is okay for people to live selfishly, destroying the lives of those around them. Sin itself has a way of carving up a person's soul. Much as with the loss of Bathsheba's first child, unrepentant sin slowly but surely destroys the sinner. (Let me make it clear, however, that having a miscarriage or losing a loved one does not mean that it happened because you sinned. We all know bad things sometimes happen to really good people.)

> Long after the most merciful among us has thrown in the towel, the Lord is still there, extending His hand of mercy and grace to people like us who don't deserve it.

The Plight of Peter and Paul

Many of us don't relate to the life of a king like David. We are way too timid to identify with a giant-killer, are too unassuming to connect with royalty or simply lack the passion that would leave a legacy that says we are a person "after God's heart." We are simple people who stumble through life, speaking out of turn and never seeming to get the answer right. Being impetuous, impatient and outspoken is our norm. For us, there is no palace, no royal processions, no famous victories. The silver spoon was a wooden spoon in our youth. We were never the teacher's pet, the coach's choice or even the most improved player. We have never been the prom queen, won a beauty pageant or received a Grammy Award. We are everyday people. The world is filled with people like us. Our heroes are underdogs and rejects. We root for the disenfranchised and the broken.

> We are everyday people. The world is filled with people like us. Our heroes are underdogs and rejects.

Welcome to the life of Peter. Through most of his early story, he is revealed as a complete screw-up. He embodies the definition of socially awkward and spiritually dysfunctional. Yet Jesus loved Peter and patiently put up with him. Jesus confronted Peter's stupidity while speaking to his destiny.

Unlike David, Peter was no courageous warrior. When a young servant girl confronted Peter just before the crucifixion about being a disciple of Christ, he denied even knowing Jesus. But that would be just one of three times that Peter would deny knowing Christ on that faithless night. Most of us would look at this as the ultimate sin. According to our standards, we would probably say that Peter had lost his faith and was never to be trusted again.

But Jesus had other plans for Peter. Look at their dialogue later:

> Jesus said to Simon Peter, "Simon son of John, do you love me more than these [more than other men love me]?"
>
> "Yes, Lord," he said, "you know that I love you."
>
> Jesus said, "Feed my lambs."
>
> Again Jesus said, "Simon son of John, do you love me?"
>
> He answered, "Yes, Lord, you know that I love you."
>
> Jesus said, "Take care of my sheep."
>
> The third time he said to him, "Simon son of John, do you love me?"
>
> Peter was hurt because Jesus asked him the third time, "Do you love me?" He said, "Lord, you know all things; you know that I love you."
>
> Jesus said, "Feed my sheep."
>
> John 21:15–17

What was Christ doing in this exchange? Remember, Peter had denied Jesus three times. Jesus was giving Peter a chance to repent for each time he had denied Him! He was also saying to Peter, "Are you going to protect the things that are most important to Me? Are you going to protect My heart?"

You would think that Christ would have said, "Peter, you have a rotten foundation. I can't build a great Church with leaders like you." Or maybe He should have said something like, "Peter, you need a sabbatical, some time off to make sure that your commitment to Me is pure." But instead, Jesus said, "I also say to you that you are Peter, and upon this rock I will build My church; and the gates of Hades will not overpower it" (Matthew 16:18 NASB). He reinforced to Peter that he was validated in Christ's eyes.

An even greater example of God's abounding grace would be the story of the apostle Paul, found in the book of Acts. Without going into much detail, before Paul was saved he was a nightmare to the Christian world, slaughtering those who preached the Good News of Jesus Christ. Paul had an encounter with the Lord while he was still a murderer. He got totally set free from his past and became one of the greatest apostles in history (see Acts 9:1–31). He wrote more than half of the New Testament, and his life is a monument to the redemptive power of Christ.

Perfect Love Casts Out Fear

By now you have probably figured out that God is not trying to punish you for your mistakes. In fact, His grace restores you back to the standard of glory that belongs to the Bride of Christ. But in order for there to be health in any relationship, it must be free from the fear of punishment. As long as you are afraid that you will be punished, love will be absent from your relationships. The Bible says, "There is no fear in love; but perfect love casts out fear, because fear involves punishment, and the one who fears is not perfected in love" (1 John 4:18 NASB). If this is true, then it is also true that "perfect fear casts out love."

Let's go back to my original question about my friend who suffered from a porn addiction. What does a guy do who has brought so much heartache on himself and his family? There is really only one thing that is going to restore them to a healthy relationship, and that is living by a new standard of love that his true repentance can create.

If your spouse was the punisher and you have repented, you have to do a reset so that you are both living by a new standard of love. It is therefore no longer okay to let him or her keep punishing you.

> If your spouse was the punisher and you have repented, you have to do a reset so that you are both living by a new standard of love.

Here is an example from my life. I remember one time when our kids were all teenagers. I got angry with Kathy in front of them and then treated her disrespectfully. The next day, I gathered the kids together in the front room and asked Kathy and each of the kids to forgive me. They all did, and we went on with our day.

About a week later, one of our boys came into the kitchen and started speaking sarcastically to Kathy. I walked in and told him, "You do not have permission to talk to your mother like that."

He said, "You were rude to Mom the other day yourself!"

I answered, "Yes, but you forgave me. Forgiveness restores the standard. When you forgave me, you gave away your right to act that same way, because your forgiveness restored me back to a place of honor. I repented. Repentance means to be restored to the pinnacle, the high place."

My son then told his mother that he was sorry, and she forgave him.

If we don't understand this principle, then the lowest point, the worst mistake or the stupidest thing we have ever done becomes our benchmark. For instance, suppose you were immoral as a teenager, and later on in life you have teenagers yourself. You can't then live by the lowest standard you set, or you won't have the confidence to correct your kids for their poor sexual choices, because you failed yourself in this area. Failures that we have repented of are no longer the standard we must bow to. When we asked God and those we hurt to forgive us, we were set back up to the high place that God assigned to us. Otherwise, the worst day of our life would become the highest place where we have the right to lead others. The truth is that forgiveness restores the standard of holiness in us and through us.

Matters of the Heart

The King James Version of Psalm 32:8 says, "I will instruct thee and teach thee in the way which thou shalt go: I will guide thee with mine eye." This is a powerful statement from the most powerful Being. Have you ever thought about why you do the things you do? Why you serve the Lord and live life according to certain standards? Is it because of the rhetoric that has been bored into you since your childhood? Or maybe because the *Left Behind* books and movies really hit home and you don't want to be the only one left alone to fight all the crazy zombies?

If your reasons for serving the Lord and laying down your life for Him are anything besides love, you have already missed the mark. Jesus said, "Many will say to me on that day, 'Lord, Lord, did we not prophesy in your name and in your name drive out demons and in your name perform many miracles?' Then I will tell them plainly, 'I never knew you'" (Matthew 7:22–23). Why didn't Jesus know them? The reason is because while they were "for" God, they were not with God. Someone once said, "The main thing is to keep the main thing the main thing!"

> If your reasons for serving the Lord and laying down your life for Him are anything besides love, you have already missed the mark.

What does this have to do with the restoration of relationships? Anytime our intimate relationships major on doing all the right things instead of having the right heart, the outcome will be a massive disconnection. When God said He would guide us with His eye, He meant that we have to be close enough and intimate enough with Him to see what He sees. We also have to care about His heart enough to be moved by His compassion. In case you have not already noticed, God is not going to force us to make good choices. He is not going to strong-arm us into a right relationship with Him. He will *guide us* into an intimate connection with Him.

The man I told you about who suffered with the porn addiction has to uphold the standard of Christ in his home, which means there is no punishment. He also has to make his connection with his family his main focus. Just as Jesus dialogued with Peter, this man's family needs to hear from him that he is going to protect their hearts. If their hearts do not affect his actions and attitudes, their relationship with him will continue to be damaged. It is the connection with his family that needs to be his guiding light and the motivation for their restoration.

I am not only talking to the people who have blown it here; I am also speaking to the people who have been abused, as I was. The same principles apply to us. Once the formerly abusive person has repented and changed the way he or she thinks, you have to look for that person to make your connection together the main goal. If you don't allow the person to restore the standard of his or her life, and if you don't see that person through God's eyes, then you will hold him/her to past mistakes through your judgments and ultimately bind both of you in a pit of destruction.

Establish the Boundaries

Establishing the boundaries of your life means that you learn how to love yourself and others in a way that promotes health. I have already said it many times, but the only relationship you can do is one that does not include punishment.

Now, if you have made a huge mess, then you are going to spend a good amount of time repenting to people and cleaning up your mess. There will be people who come to you a year later and say, "I'm still having a hard time because of what you've done." This is not the time to say back to them, "Well, I'm a changed person, so you just need to get over it!" This is the time to go back in your heart to the place of repentance you originally presented to them and do it all over again, if that is what they need.

I realize this can get really tricky, because often it is a spouse or a child who cannot get over something and who continually brings up the issue, refusing to change the way he or she sees you. Ultimately, this hurting family member is not looking for restoration in your relationship, but for justice through punishment. In this case, you will have to let this person know that his or her feelings and hurt are valid, but that the only way to restore the relationship is to extend the same forgiveness to you that Jesus extended to both of you.

In establishing boundaries that reset a standard of love, it is important that you don't send a big fat message that because Jesus forgave you, you are now free to act however you want. Rather, the message you want to send is that you know your actions and choices have caused a ton of damage. You have discovered the root issues of your heart that caused you to behave the way you did, and you are going to protect the person's heart by changing the way you think.

> In establishing boundaries that reset a standard of love, it is important that you don't send a big fat message that because Jesus forgave you, you are now free to act however you want.

Like the Lone Ranger in the Wild West, old habits die hard. In establishing the boundaries and setting the standard of your life, you will have to be patient with the environment around you as people struggle to trust you again and see you differently.

Communication Is King

I worked with the former porn addict for months, helping him move out of the role of being the receptacle of his family's punishment. I taught him how to communicate to them so that the way they were talking to him and treating him did not feel punishing. I also taught him that his family had very real fears and needs that he must address. When his wife would begin to punish him, he learned how to stop her kindly and say, "I'm feeling punished. Is there a way that you could rephrase that statement, or is there something that you need to get from me without belittling me?"

Over and over again, this repentant husband and father would have to take a stand for himself, while also making his wife's heart a huge priority. Without setting new boundaries, he had no way of actually taking care of his family. His family did not need a broken-down man; they needed a man with a standard, a man who cared about their hearts and who was going to teach them that just as he was valuable, they were valuable, too.

At first, this man's newfound standard was met with fierce opposition, because change is almost as scary as death. His wife had always been the punisher in the relationship, and he had never set a boundary that disallowed her abuse toward him. Over time and through lots of tears, he began to learn how to hear his wife's heart and also to uphold the standard in their house by using statements like, "You sound really frustrated. Is there a way I can help you?" Or, "I'm trying to hear what you're saying, but when you throw judgment at me, it makes me want to protect myself from you. Is there a way that you can say what you're feeling so that I don't have to feel defensive, and so that I can really hear you?"

Sometimes when his wife was feeling really frustrated and was unable to change the way she was talking, he would have to try to stay in the conversation by saying something like, "Are you really trying to say . . . ?" Then he would reiterate whatever it was he thought she was trying to communicate. Ultimately, his actions and approach sent her the message that he really wanted to hear and validate her heart and lower her anxiety, but at the same time, that he was unwilling to continue the dysfunctional cycle they had created in their lives.

By persistently practicing good communication, you can push past your fear of being locked into your past, and you can give people a way to love you as you are now. Whether you know it or not, you are the one who teaches the people in your life how lovable you are. You show others how to treat you by the way you care for yourself, and by the way you allow others to treat you. All these things are your responsibility. No matter how wrong you have been in the past, Christ's forgiveness gives you permission to restore the standard in your life.

REFLECT

1. Is there any area in your life in which the fear of punishment is keeping you from being honest, open or real?

2. Where do you think your fear of being punished originated? If it came from a religious spirit, have you now accepted that you are valuable enough to be worth others extending to you the same forgiveness Christ extended to all of us?

3. If your fear of punishment originated with another person, what have you done to reset the standard in your life? In other words, have you communicated that while you want to restore the relationship, you are unwilling to live in a cycle of abuse?

4. What kind of loving communication can you use to set a new standard of love with those people whom you have hurt? In other words, how can you establish with them that you want forgiveness and restoration, but that abuse and punishment are no longer welcome?

TWELVE

Hope, the Final Frontier

The side effects of my broken marriage created more trauma in my soul than I could ever have imagined because I was an *all in*, completely devoted, no plan B, this-is-forever kind of guy. Call me naïve or inexperienced, but I was so full of hope for us that I only envisioned a fantastic future. Consequently, our divorce did not just break my heart; it shattered my childlike trust in God and sunk my soul deep into the sea of hopelessness. Subsequently, I unknowingly protected myself from more pain by making an inner vow never to hope again.

Solomon described my situation perfectly when he wrote, "Hope deferred makes the heart sick, but a longing fulfilled is a tree of life" (Proverbs 13:12). Postponing the things I hoped for was not making my heart sick; it was deferring hope itself that was killing me. The fact that I had decided to stop hoping actually imprisoned my soul and tormented my heart. My challenge with hope was that it required risk, and thus the possibility of failure. I suddenly understood why even brave people often cling to their pitiful past to avoid the painful possibility of a derailed future. This is the plight of self-preservation—a meager existence and an incredibly boring life. Our big dreams whittled down to mere survival as we sit alone in the dark, "safe" cave of obscurity, licking our wounds and cursing our future.

> My challenge with hope was that it required risk, and thus the possibility of failure.

Looking back, I can see that in the midst of my pain I had forgotten the lifetime of victories I already had won in the Lord. I was like the Israelites whom God had miraculously freed from the heavy-handed Egyptians after four hundred years of bondage, who then only clung to the fear of their demise. You might remember the story of how Pharaoh's army of horses and chariots pursued the Israelites with deadly intent. Trapped between the Red Sea and an angry Egyptian army, the Israelites watched God push back the waters and usher them through the sea on dry land. The Egyptian army pursued them fiercely, but God released the Red Sea against these enemies and drowned their entire army!

Saved from the Egyptians, the Israelites began their forty-year walk around the wilderness, warmed by the fire of God at night and cooled by the shadow of His supernatural cloud during the day. Moreover, God literally fed them with angel food (manna) every day. Yet when faced with their ultimate destination, the Promised Land, they refused to go in because they did not trust God to defeat the giants in the land.

Imagine what it must have felt like to finally arrive at the border after four hundred years of bondage and forty years of wandering in a dusty wilderness, only to find that there was more opposition to face in their Promised Land. As it turned out, the Israelites' faithlessness caused them to become disheartened. They were emotionally, mentally, physically and spiritually worn out, with no hope. . . .

It is so easy to point the finger of judgment at the Israelites' stupidity, especially after all the miracles God had done for them. He had proven to them time and time again that they were His divinely protected people. Yet the truth is, we often have the same problem they did. We can be just like the people of Israel, who became jaded with God and spent their lives wandering in the desert. What God intends as a blessing in our lives can ultimately become our demise because, like the Israelites, we literally cannot see our future in light of our traumatic past.

Remember, God had saved Israel from Egypt, yet the Israelites never left Egypt behind in their hearts. Consequently, an entire generation of men and women died never having obtained what was promised. It is so important that we learn from those faithless Israelites and keep our eye on the prize, especially in the midst of our trials and tribulations.

The Key to Hope

Perseverance is the key to keeping hope alive. Perseverance is simply faith that refuses to give up. When the circumstances are dire and the people become downcast, faith seeps through the pores of the principled and pounds a pillar of possibility into the hearts of the hopeless. Persistent hope inevitably dictates the day for those who will hold onto faith . . . bringing within the realm of possibility the undoable feat, the unknowable task and the unimaginable miracle.

This reminds me of a story that emerged a few years ago from one of the largest gold mines in America, which is located in Round Mountain, Nevada. The miners digging in the mine struck the mother lode, one of the largest veins of gold ever discovered in recorded history. As the miners excavated around the massive gold vein, they made another discovery. They found a tunnel several miles long that had been dug around the time of the gold rush and had been abandoned just one hundred feet from the mother lode! Think about it: Those early miners had spent years digging in a tunnel, looking for gold, only to quit a day too soon.

Tragic? Yes! Common? Absolutely. The same kind of thing is all too common in our lives today. This is what happens when we lose sight of God's heart for us. God's intention has always been clear. Jeremiah said it best: "'I know the plans that I have for you,' declares the Lord, 'plans for welfare and not for calamity to give you a future and a hope'" (Jeremiah 29:11 NASB). There is no magic trick to staying in the will of the Lord; it is literally a choice. We get to choose in whom we will believe. Will we believe our circumstances, or will we put our faith in the Lord? This is the million-dollar question—the mother lode of the Kingdom of God.

In the world, seeing is believing. In the Kingdom, believing is seeing. Faith is not the absence of facts; it is the presence of conviction. There is actually no such thing as blind faith, because faith sees what is not yet visible, hopes for what is not yet viable and trusts in what others don't value. Faith is the bridge between what is and what will be.

> There is no magic trick to staying in the will of the Lord; it is literally a choice. We get to choose in whom we will believe.

Faith is not a mindless exercise in futility; it is a Spirit-led adventure into our Promised Land. The question is not, Do we have faith? The question is, Where did we put our faith? Everyone has faith, but if we don't invest it in the Infinite One, then we spend it on finite solutions that ultimately fail.

It is important to understand that fear is faith in the wrong god. Think about it: You never experience fear unless you *believe* in a negative outcome, or unless you begin to dread something going awry in your life. On the other hand, faith in God produces the fruit of the Spirit, which is love, joy, peace, patience, kindness, goodness, faithfulness, gentleness and self-control (see Galatians

5:22–23). These attributes give us the ability to thrive in every season of life.

Rats

Choosing to trust God and fan the flame of hope in our lives has been scientifically verified to improve our lives. One of my favorite proofs of this comes from an experiment done back in the 1950s by Johns Hopkins scientist Curt Paul Richter. He discovered that rats could swim and stay alive in high-sided buckets of circulating water for only about 15 minutes. After that, they would give up the ghost and sink. Curt made an incredible discovery, however, when he decided to start rescuing the exhausted rodents to give them a short rest before returning them back to the water. Miraculously, the rats that once upon a time would probably have sunk after only 15 minutes somehow managed to swim for 60 hours. That is 240 times longer than rats that were not temporarily rescued! How is that even possible? Dr. Richter concluded that the rescued rats were given hope. Energized by hope, they swam around thinking they would be rescued again, even if it meant keeping it up for 60 hours.

This story is both fascinating and confirming to me. Throughout my years of counseling, I have observed the role that hope plays in people's ability to get well. For instance, some years ago I worked with a married couple in which the husband had engaged in multiple affairs. As you can imagine, the situation was dire. At first, the counseling actually seemed to make the situation worse since each time we met, another horrible story of unfaithfulness surfaced. I literally could not believe this man's wife was still showing up to the sessions. As if that were not impressive enough, in spite of her husband's multiple affairs, she came to the meetings to find out how she could improve as both a woman and a wife.

To this day, I have never witnessed another demonstration of faith and hope like this wife showed in such a situation. Usually, the innocent party *only* focuses on the spouse's violations and the erosion of trust. But not this woman! She had made up her mind that regardless of the facts, she was going to fight for her marriage by improving herself personally, while setting clear and healthy boundaries with her husband.

Honestly, this woman was not even sure that her husband was going to choose to come back into the relationship, but she realized that his staying or leaving was not something she could control. She just stayed focused on God's unfathomable goodness, and her soul rested confidently in His love for her. Some really long, tough years passed as the Lord slowly and completely restored their marriage, which has now become a hallmark of love and affection, a living testimony to God's miraculous ability to restore anybody. I attribute their restoration 100 percent to their ability to hold onto hope in the midst of the darkest days of their relationship.

Feeding Hope

The question is, How do you cultivate this kind of life-changing hope in your soul? That is actually a great question. The apostle John helped us answer it when he wrote, "The testimony of Jesus is the spirit of prophecy" (Revelation 19:10 NKJV). This literally means that whatever good thing(s) God did for someone else, He will do for you. In other words, their testimony is your prophecy . . . your future success. Remember, God is no respecter of persons, so if He did something amazing for someone else, He is surely willing to do it for you, too. Thinking about this is one of the best ways to cultivate hope and build faith in our lives.

Yet another powerful tool that feeds hope in our hearts is to recall what God has said about our future. The Bible calls these future God ideas "prophecies." Prophecies are God's plans and desires for our future. For years, Pastor Bill Johnson has carried 3x5 cards everywhere he goes, with the prophecies God has spoken to or about him transcribed on them. (He now has them on his iPad.) He reviews these prophecies often so that he remains conscious of what God thinks about his life and future. Whenever Bill is having a hard day, instead of drowning in the hopeless facts of a particular circumstance, he goes straight to the cards and strengthens himself in God's words to him.

Meditating on God's acts, His perspective and His Word is the secret of continually living in a place of hope. In fact, God Himself gave His servant Joshua this advice: "This Book of the Law shall not depart from your mouth, but you shall meditate in it day and night, that you may observe to do according to all that is written in it. For then you will make your way prosperous, and then you will have good success" (Joshua 1:8 NKJV).

Victims to Victors

Sometimes instead of cultivating hope, we foster self-pity and a victim mentality in ourselves, reasoning that everyone else has it so much better than we do. It might actually be true that we have been handed a tougher lot in life than others. Yet feeling sorry for ourselves will not empower us to live a better life. What will inspire us to victory is to find people who also have inherited a challenging life and who have become successful in God, in spite of their circumstances.

In light of this, one of my heroes is Abraham Lincoln. We Americans see him as a father of our nation and a master of perseverance and hope. We know him as one of the most popular presidents in American history. Yet it is Abraham Lincoln's list of troubles and failures that is one of the most impressive beacons of light and hope in the world. You can find more than one record of his many failures recounted online and elsewhere, but here is a partial list:

- 1818—His mother died when he was nine years old.

- 1831—His business failed.
- 1832—He lost a bid for a minor post in the legislature.
- 1833—He failed in business again.
- 1833—His possessions were seized when he was unable to pay off his debts.
- 1835—His wife-to-be died.
- 1843—He failed to receive his party's nomination for Congress.
- 1853—His son died.
- 1854—He fell six votes short of securing an open seat in the Senate.

In spite of all his troubles and failures, Abraham Lincoln persevered. Talk about a guy who knew how to get up when he was knocked down! The result was that ultimately, he was twice elected president of the United States, first in 1860, and then again in 1864. Add to this the fact that he served as president during the Civil War, the most trying time in America's history.

Thousands of years ago, Solomon penned these words: "Where there is no vision, the people are unrestrained" (Proverbs 29:18 NASB). There is so much truth held inside these simple words. Abe Lincoln clung to his vision in the midst of the darkest nights of his soul. It is vision that keeps hope alive in us. Hopelessness is a serial killer. Without hope, we have no faith. And without faith, we cannot please God, and the world becomes a miserable place to live.

God is the master of search and rescue. When everything looks bleak in our lives, we just need to look over our shoulder and we will find Him there. When Daniel was thrown into the lions' den and everything seemed dark and hopeless, God saved him. When Shadrach, Meshach and Abednego were tossed into the fiery furnace, Jesus set them free. When God found a man so bound with lies that he was murdering Christians, the Savior encountered him on the road to Damascus and changed his name from Saul to Paul, transforming him into one of the greatest men of God ever to grace this planet.

> Abe Lincoln clung to his vision in the midst of the darkest nights of his soul. It is vision that keeps hope alive in us.

The stories go on and on of God's amazing ability to transform people. There was the demonized man in the country of the Gadarenes. There was Lazarus, who had been dead four days. There was Mary Magdalene, the prostitute. There was Joseph, who was sold into slavery but became a prince. And there was David, who killed a giant with a rock. There is no hand you are dealt that God cannot use to win.

Whatever happens in your life, remember this: Jesus is the master of making palaces out of pitfalls. It is never too late for Him to redeem your situation. Throughout all the battles I have fought both in my personal journey and in counseling others, and throughout all the battles my dad has fought for himself and in helping others, we have become completely convinced that no matter how far you have fallen or how big a mess you have made out of your life, God is "able to do immeasurably more than all we ask or imagine" (Ephesians 3:20). He specializes in the impossible, and despite how you are feeling, He is for you. And since He is for you, you can win the war within!

1. What area of your life could you use more hope in? Reflect again on Jeremiah 29:11, "'I know the plans that I have for you,' declares the Lord, 'plans for welfare and not for calamity to give you a future and a hope'" (Jeremiah 29:11 NASB). What does this Scripture do to your perspective on the area you identified where you could use more hope?

2. Make a list of testimonies about the things God has done in your life already. What effect does this list have on your level of hope?

3. If you have partnered with hopelessness, take time to repent and break that partnership.

4. Now partner with hope and write out a clear vision for this season in your life.

Jason Vallotton is the pastoral care overseer of Bethel Church in Redding, California, and is a sought-after counselor, teacher and speaker. Jason also oversees Bethel Church's men's ministry, with a passion to see "the hearts of fathers turn back to their children." He served at Bethel School of Supernatural Ministry for over ten years and has co-authored three books with his dad, Kris: *The Supernatural Power of Forgiveness*, *Moral Revolution*, and *Outrageous Courage*. Jason and his wife, Lauren, live in Redding with their four wonderful children.

Kris Vallotton is the senior associate leader of Bethel Church in Redding, California, and is cofounder of Bethel School of Supernatural Ministry (BSSM). Kris travels internationally, training and equipping people to fulfill their divine purpose successfully. He is a bestselling author, having written more than a dozen books and training manuals to help prepare believers for life in the Kingdom. He has a diverse background in business, counseling, consulting, pastoring and teaching, which gives him unique leadership insights and perspectives. Kris has a passion to use his experience and his prophetic gift to assist world leaders in achieving their goals and accomplishing their mission. He is the author of the popular blog *Kris Vallotton: Raw, Real & Relevant*. Kris has been married to his wife, Kathy, since 1975, and they have four children and many grandchildren.

You May Also Like . . .

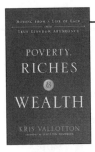

In this eye-opening study of what the Bible really says about money, poverty, riches and wealth, Kris Vallotton will shake up what you thought you knew, showing that Kingdom prosperity always begins from the inside out. When you learn to cultivate a mindset of abundance, you will begin to experience the wealth of heaven in every area of your life.

Poverty, Riches and Wealth

At this pivotal hour, when evil dominates the headlines and the media persecutes any dissenters, God is searching for men and women who will take a stand in His name. Even now, He is readying a heavy rain of revival. Here is the guidance you need to become a vessel that catches the downpour of the Spirit's rain—and helps release the Kingdom like a flood.

Heavy Rain

Go deeper into the heart of one of the most crucial, compelling and controversial topics today: the office of prophet. In this definitive guide, Kris Vallotton offers foundational teaching and provides critical advanced training. You will come away empowered and equipped with the knowledge and skills needed for this vital supernatural ministry.

School of the Prophets

Also from Kris Vallotton

God's crowning creation in the Garden was Woman. Yet the state of our world belies her true beauty and purpose. In this eye-opening book, Kris Vallotton reveals God's true plan and purpose for all women—both in the Church and throughout creation. As sons and daughters of the King, it's time for men and women to work together to restore God's original design for biblical partnership.

Fashioned to Reign

Sharing his deeply personal story of demonic bondage, torment and ultimate deliverance, Kris Vallotton turns the idea of spiritual warfare as we know it on its head. He reveals the diabolical lies and strategies of the enemy and arms you with a bold new battle plan. Now you can win the invisible battle against sin and the enemy. Victory is within your grasp. Will you take hold?

Spirit Wars